CIRCUS ECONOMICS

The Hidden Financial Empire Behind Chariot Racing Syndicates

MARCUS VERDINEAU

This book is a work of nonfiction. It draws on ancient primary sources and modern scholarship as described in the Note on Sources included at the end of this book. Every reasonable effort has been made to ensure the accuracy of the historical information presented, though readers should understand that the study of antiquity often involves incomplete evidence and ongoing scholarly debate.

CONTENTS

AUTHOR'S NOTE

There is a version of Roman history that most of us already know without ever having studied it. It arrives through film and television, through half remembered lessons and museum placards, and it goes roughly like this. Rome was an empire of soldiers and senators, of aqueducts and gladiators, of emperors who were either brilliant or insane and often both at once. It is not a wrong history. It is simply an incomplete one, and the missing piece is larger than most people realize.

For nearly a thousand years, the single most popular form of entertainment in the Roman world was not the gladiatorial combat that dominates modern imagination. It was chariot racing. The Circus Maximus in Rome could seat a quarter of a million people, more than the entire population of most Roman provincial capitals, and it did so on a near weekly basis for centuries. When historians tally the days on the Roman calendar given over to public spectacle, chariot racing claims more of them than any other event, gladiatorial games included. The four racing factions, known by their colors of Red, White, Blue, and Green, commanded a loyalty so fierce that it shaped urban riots, influenced imperial politics, and in one catastrophic week in the year 532, nearly burned Constantinople to the ground.

I did not set out to write a book about chariots. I set out to understand how a preindustrial economy without stock markets, insurance companies, or centralized banking managed to sustain an entertainment industry of staggering scale for the better part of a millennium. The answer, once I started pulling on the thread, led directly to the racetrack. The horse breeding operations that supplied the circus stretched from the plains of Iberia to the highlands of Cappadocia, moving animals across the length of the Mediterranean world in a logistics network that would not look wildly unfamiliar to a modern livestock exporter. The stable owners who ran the four factions, men known in Latin as domini factionum, controlled fortunes that rivaled senatorial estates while sitting, technically, outside the senatorial class altogether. The charioteers themselves, most of them enslaved at the start of their careers, could retire as some of the wealthiest individuals in the ancient Mediterranean, a fact so well documented in surviving inscriptions that we can reconstruct, race by race, exactly how one man earned the equivalent of a small province's annual tax revenue.

This is not a book that treats chariot racing as a curiosity or a footnote to more serious history. It treats the sport as what it actually was: one of the largest and most sophisticated commercial enterprises of the ancient world, built on horse breeding markets, labor systems, gambling networks, public subsidy, and celebrity culture that operated with a logic any modern reader will find uncomfortably recognizable. The men who ran the factions were not sportsmen in the amateur sense that later centuries would romanticize. They were businessmen, and shrewd ones, operating in an environment where the difference between a good horse and a great one could be measured in fortunes.

I have tried, throughout this book, to stay as close as possible to what the evidence actually says. Roman antiquity did not leave behind balance sheets in the modern sense, and anyone who claims to reconstruct exact profit margins for a faction in the second century is engaged in more speculation than scholarship. What we do have is remarkable in its own right: inscriptions carved in stone by charioteers proud enough of their earnings to have the figures preserved for eternity, legal texts wrestling with the economic status of enslaved athletes, satirical poetry mocking the excesses of faction spending, and the physical remains of breeding farms, training compounds, and the tracks themselves. Where the evidence is solid, I have built on it directly. Where it thins out, as it inevitably does in places, I have said so rather than papering over the gaps with invented certainty.

The story that emerges is not simply an economic curiosity. It is a story about what happens when a society decides that entertainment deserves the same seriousness of investment as war or infrastructure, and about the men, mostly forgotten by name today, who built fortunes by understanding that better than anyone else around them. Some of those names survive only as letters carved into weathered stone. A few, like the charioteer Gaius Appuleius Diocles, left behind enough detail that we can trace their working lives almost race by race. All of them were part of a machine that ran, quite literally, on money, long before anyone had a word for the kind of economy they were building.

I hope this book restores some of that machine to view. The dust has settled over the Circus Maximus for more than a thousand years, but the ledgers, in the places where they survive, still have a great deal to say.

CHAPTER ONE

THE VALLEY BETWEEN TWO HILLS

The floor of the valley was mud before it was marble.

Long before anyone thought to call it the greatest stadium the ancient world would ever build, the low ground between the Aventine and Palatine hills was simply a floodplain, cut by a stream that the early inhabitants of the site called the Murcia and prone, like most river bottoms, to turning into a shallow lake whenever the Tiber rose. It was an unlikely place to build anything permanent, let alone a structure that would eventually stretch more than six hundred meters end to end and hold, at its largest, something in the range of a quarter of a million people. Yet this is precisely where the Romans chose to build the Circus Maximus, and understanding why they chose that spot, and what they built there over the following centuries, is the necessary starting point for understanding everything that follows in this book. You cannot study the economics of an industry without first understanding the physical plant on which that industry was built, and in the case of Roman chariot racing, that physical plant was, by any measure, one of the most ambitious construction projects in human history up to that point.

Roman tradition credited the earliest circus at this site to the kings, specifically to Tarquinius Priscus in the sixth century before the common era, though as with most Roman origin stories involving the monarchy, the details are more legend than documented fact. What can be said with more confidence is that the valley was used for horse and chariot competition from a very early period in Rome's history, tied initially to religious festivals honoring Consus, a god associated with grain storage and, by extension, with the horse races held in his honor at harvest time. This religious framing matters more than it might first appear. Chariot racing in Rome never fully shed its origins as a sacred event, and this had direct economic consequences that will recur throughout this book. Because the races were, at least in official terms, religious observances rather than purely secular entertainment, the Roman state had both the justification and, over time, the obligation to fund them publicly. A government could tax its citizens to pay for something framed as an offering to the gods in a way that would have been far harder to justify for pure amusement. The line between sacred obligation and public entertainment blurred almost immediately and never fully separated again for the entire history of the institution.

The earliest circus structures were modest by the standards of what would come later. Wooden seating, raised on temporary or semi-permanent frames, accommodated the upper classes who wished to watch in some comfort, while a wider mass of spectators stood or sat on the natural slopes of the two flanking hills. This arrangement, primitive as it sounds, established a social pattern that would persist for the entire life of the institution: proximity to the track correlated directly with social status and, just as importantly, with the price a spectator or their patron might pay to secure a seat. Even in these earliest phases, before any of the four great racing factions had taken organized shape, the Circus was already functioning as a stratified economic space, a fact easy to overlook when the popular imagination pictures ancient spectacle as a kind of universal democratic gathering. It was nothing of the sort. The best seats were finite, valuable, and controlled, and that scarcity would remain a defining economic feature of the venue for as long as it operated.

Expansion came in stages, each one driven by a combination of political ambition, genuine engineering advancement, and, crucially, the growing commercial reality that a bigger circus meant more revenue opportunities for everyone with a financial stake in the games. Livy and other Roman historians record periodic additions and renovations across the Republican period: new seating for senatorial families, marked divisions for different social orders, and gradual replacement of wood with more durable stone and concrete in the lower tiers. By the time of Julius Caesar in the first century before the common era, the Circus had been substantially rebuilt to hold an estimated one hundred and fifty thousand spectators, an almost incomprehensible figure for the ancient world, dwarfing the capacity of the Colosseum that would later rise on the other side of the city. Subsequent emperors kept adding to it. After a catastrophic fire in the year 64 of the common era, one that began, according to Tacitus, in the very shops and stalls clustered around the arena's perimeter and went on to consume large sections of Rome itself, the Circus was rebuilt on an even grander scale. By the reign of Trajan in the early second century, ancient sources describe a capacity approaching two hundred thousand, and under later emperors, particularly Constantine in the fourth century, estimates climb as high as a quarter of a million, though modern historians treat the upper end of these figures with appropriate caution, since ancient authors were not above a bit of imperial flattery when describing the scale of a ruler's public works.

What is not in dispute is the sheer physical footprint of the finished structure. Archaeological surveys place the Circus Maximus at roughly six hundred and twenty meters in length and somewhere between one hundred and eighteen and one hundred and fifty meters in width, depending on which phase of construction one is measuring. To put that in terms a modern reader can hold in their head, the track itself was longer than five and a half modern American football fields laid end to end, and its seating tiers rose, in the final Constantinian phase, to a height of around twenty eight meters, the rough equivalent of a nine story building. This was not merely large. It was, for over a thousand years, the largest purpose built entertainment venue that human beings had ever constructed, and no stadium built anywhere on earth would exceed its seating capacity until the modern era of steel and reinforced concrete made such feats of engineering unremarkable.

Consider what a structure of that scale demanded, purely as a matter of logistics and finance, and the outlines of an entire economy begin to emerge before we have even mentioned a single charioteer, horse, or wager. A venue built to hold hundreds of thousands of people required a construction labor force numbering in the thousands, sustained over years or decades. It required a continuous supply chain for building materials: quarried stone, kiln fired brick, timber hauled from forests that, by the imperial period, were often located hundreds of miles away as the closer supplies were exhausted. It required an ongoing maintenance budget, since a wooden upper tier exposed to Roman weather and the crush of enormous crowds needed constant repair, and even the stone lower tiers suffered from flooding when the Tiber overtopped its banks, which it did with some regularity throughout Roman history. And once built, the structure demanded an entirely separate category of ongoing expenditure simply to fill it with events worth watching: horses, chariots, drivers, staff, and the prize money that gave charioteers a reason to risk their lives on the sand.

None of this was cheap, and none of it was accidental. The Roman state and, later, individual emperors treated investment in the Circus Maximus as a form of political currency in its own right. The famous phrase attributed to the satirist Juvenal, describing a Roman public grown complacent and controllable through the twin provision of bread and circuses, panem et circenses, was not merely a clever turn of phrase. It was an accurate diagnosis of a deliberate governing strategy that Roman elites pursued for centuries, one in which the funding of spectacular public entertainment functioned as a direct substitute for, or supplement to, more conventional forms of political legitimacy. A senator or, later, an emperor who funded lavish games purchased goodwill from a public that might otherwise have grown restive over food shortages, tax burdens, or military setbacks. This is an economic relationship as much as a political one, and it is the first of many places in this book where the language of modern finance, subsidy, public investment, and return on political capital, turns out to describe ancient Roman behavior with startling precision.

The valley itself deserves a closer look, because its physical geography shaped the economic activity that would eventually surround it in ways that are easy to miss if one thinks of the Circus Maximus only as a racetrack. The site sat close to the Tiber and to the network of roads converging on Rome from the south and west, making it a natural hub for the movement of goods and animals into the city. Stables and training grounds for the racing factions clustered in the surrounding districts, alongside markets, taverns, and lodging houses that catered to the enormous seasonal influx of visitors drawn to Rome specifically for major race days. Ancient sources describe the areas immediately outside the Circus as densely commercial, packed with the small shops, food vendors, and services that any large gathering of people generates almost spontaneously. This commercial penumbra surrounding the Circus was itself a significant economic zone, one that generated tax revenue, employed a substantial workforce, and depended entirely on the continued popularity of the races for its survival. When we ask, as this book repeatedly will, how large the chariot racing economy actually was, we cannot restrict our accounting to the prize purses won by charioteers or the profits of the faction owners. We have to include the entire ecosystem of ancillary commerce that grew up around the venue, much of which has left far fainter traces in the historical record than the celebrated names of famous drivers, but which almost certainly moved as much or more money in aggregate.

The Tiber itself deserves particular mention in any account of the Circus Maximus's physical history, since the river's periodic flooding represented a recurring and genuinely significant threat to the venue's structural integrity throughout its many centuries of operation. Ancient sources record numerous instances of flood damage to the lower tiers of seating, closest to the valley floor and therefore most vulnerable when the Tiber overtopped its banks, a hazard the original builders had accepted as an unavoidable consequence of siting the venue in a natural floodplain in the first place. Each significant flood necessitated repair expenditure, adding yet another recurring category of cost to the ongoing maintenance budget this chapter has already described, and the pattern of damage and repair across the centuries offers modern archaeologists a useful, if unintentional, stratigraphic record of the venue's long structural history, with successive layers of flood deposited silt and subsequent repair work marking the passage of particularly severe inundations across the many centuries the Circus remained in active use. This vulnerability to flooding was never fully engineered away, even as the Romans grew increasingly sophisticated in their hydraulic engineering more generally, a testament to just how firmly the location itself, chosen many centuries earlier for reasons of religious tradition and available open space rather than optimal drainage, had become fixed as the site of Rome's premier entertainment venue by the time later emperors might otherwise have considered relocating to more naturally secure ground.

It is worth pausing here to address a question that any careful reader should be asking: how much of this can we actually verify, and how much are we inferring from indirect evidence? This is a fair challenge, and it deserves an honest answer rather than the kind of breezy certainty that popular history sometimes substitutes for genuine scholarship. The physical dimensions of the Circus Maximus rest on solid archaeological ground, confirmed by excavation and by the consistent testimony of multiple ancient authors writing at different periods, even where their specific capacity estimates diverge somewhat depending on which phase of construction they were describing. The broader claims about ancillary commerce, the taverns and shops and lodging houses, rest on a combination of archaeological survey of the surrounding districts, references in Roman legal and satirical texts, and comparison with better documented commercial patterns around other major Roman public venues. This is legitimate historical inference, but it is inference nonetheless, and this book will try to be transparent throughout about where the evidence is direct and where it is reconstructed from circumstantial but reasonable indicators. The financial empire built around chariot racing left behind far less in the way of formal accounting than a modern reader might hope for. What it left instead is a scattered but genuinely rich body of inscriptions, legal rulings, satirical commentary, and physical remains, and piecing these together honestly, without overstating what any single piece of evidence can bear, is the task this entire book sets out to accomplish.

The valley between the Aventine and Palatine hills, then, was never simply a racetrack. From its earliest religious origins through its final monumental form under the later emperors, it was the physical anchor for a commercial and political ecosystem that touched nearly every level of Roman society, from the enslaved stable hands mucking out horse pens before dawn to the emperor himself, whose presence at the games was as much a calculated act of political theater as it was a personal indulgence. Understanding the scale of what the Romans built in that valley, and why they kept building it larger across centuries, is the essential foundation for everything that follows. The four factions that would eventually dominate the sport, the breeding networks that supplied their horses, the charioteers who risked death for fortune, and the vast betting economy that grew up around every race, all of it depended on the existence of a venue capacious enough, and permanent enough, to sustain an industry of this size for the better part of a millennium. Rome did not stumble into building the largest entertainment venue in the ancient world. It built the Circus Maximus deliberately, expanded it deliberately, and funded it deliberately, because the men who governed Rome understood something that modern sports economists would take two thousand years to formalize into an academic discipline: that a well built stadium is not merely a place to watch a contest. It is an engine, and like any engine, it generates far more activity around itself than the event it was nominally built to house.

That engine is the subject of this book. Before we can follow the money into the breeding farms of Hispania, the counting rooms of the faction managers, or the betting stalls where fortunes changed hands on a single race, we needed first to see the valley itself, mud turned to marble, wooden benches turned to a colossus of stone that could swallow a quarter of a million people and somehow still leave them wanting more. The next chapter turns to the men who first understood how to organize that appetite into something resembling a business, and the four colors under which they built it.

CHAPTER TWO

THE COLORS OF MONEY

Four colors. That is all it took to organize an industry that would eventually command the loyalty of an entire empire and the working lives of thousands of people scattered from Britain to North Africa. Red, White, Blue, and Green. By the middle of the first century of the common era, these four factions, known in Latin as factiones, had absorbed or eliminated every rival operation and settled into a duopoly of influence that would define professional chariot racing for the remainder of Roman and Byzantine history. To understand how Roman chariot racing functioned as an economic system, one has to start here, with the strange and largely unprecedented corporate structure that grew up around these four colors, because nothing about the way the factions operated resembles the romantic image of amateur athletic competition that later centuries liked to project backward onto antiquity. These were businesses, run by businessmen, for profit, and the racing itself was, in a very real sense, simply the product they were selling.

The origins of the color system are genuinely uncertain, and ancient sources themselves offer competing explanations rather than a single agreed account. The early Christian writer

Tertullian, writing at the end of the second century in a treatise condemning public spectacles as morally corrosive, claimed that only two factions existed at first, the White and the Red, associated respectively with winter and summer, before the Blue and Green were added to complete an association with the four seasons: Blue for autumn and sky, Green for spring and earth. Whether this seasonal symbolism reflects genuine early Roman religious thinking or a later rationalization imposed on an already established system is difficult to determine with certainty, and modern historians remain divided on the question. What is not in doubt is that by the time we have solid documentary evidence, from the late Republic onward, all four factions existed as fully formed commercial operations with their own stables, staff, equipment, and fan bases, competing directly against one another in every major race held in the Circus Maximus and, eventually, in circuses built throughout the provinces.

The man who ran a faction, called in Latin a dominus factionis, occupied a peculiar and genuinely interesting position within Roman social hierarchy. Most faction owners belonged to the equestrian order, the class of Roman citizens who ranked immediately below the senatorial elite in formal status but who were frequently their equals or superiors in raw wealth. This placement was not accidental. Roman law and custom placed certain restrictions on the direct commercial activities senators could engage in, restrictions rooted in an old aristocratic prejudice that treated hands on commerce, as opposed to income from land, as somewhat beneath senatorial dignity. The equestrian order faced no such restriction, and men of that class filled the ranks of tax farmers, shipping magnates, and, as it happens, chariot racing entrepreneurs throughout the Republic and into the early Empire. Running a faction required exactly the kind of large scale capital investment, logistical coordination, and risk tolerance that equestrian businessmen specialized in elsewhere in the Roman economy, and the profits, when the operation succeeded, could be substantial enough to rival even senatorial fortunes built on land and provincial administration.

What, precisely, did a faction owner actually own and operate? The answer, reconstructed from a combination of legal texts, inscriptions, and archaeological remains of faction stable complexes excavated in Rome, is a surprisingly extensive commercial enterprise. At the center sat the stables themselves, called stabula, which housed not merely the racing horses but an entire supporting population of grooms, veterinarians, farriers, harness makers, and general laborers, many of them enslaved, who kept the animals fed, trained, and healthy enough to compete. Surviving inscriptions record an entire hierarchy of specialized staff within a single faction: there were sarcinatores who managed equipment and tack, medici who tended to injured horses and, when necessary, injured drivers, and a rank of trainers responsible for developing young horses and novice charioteers into competition ready athletes. This was not a small operation staffed casually as race days approached. It was a year round enterprise employing what inscriptional evidence suggests could be several hundred individuals attached to a single major faction in Rome at any given time, a workforce comparable in scale to a substantial Roman manufacturing operation or agricultural estate.

Beyond the stables in Rome itself, faction operations extended into an entire supply network for horses, a subject this book will examine in far greater depth in the following chapter, but which deserves at least a preliminary mention here because it illustrates the geographic scope of what a faction actually managed. Horses destined for the Circus Maximus were bred on specialized farms in regions renowned for producing quality racing stock: Hispania in the western Mediterranean, Cappadocia in central Anatolia, and parts of North Africa near Carthage all developed reputations, attested in ancient agricultural writers like Columella, as premier sources of circus horses. A faction owner or his agents needed to negotiate purchases or long term supply arrangements with breeders in these distant regions, arrange for the animals to be transported, often by sea, to Italy, and then integrate newly acquired horses into training programs that could take years before an animal was ready to compete at the highest level. This was, in the fullest sense of the term, an international commercial supply chain, coordinated across a geographic range that would not have been unfamiliar to a modern logistics manager, even if the tools available to a second century Roman stable master were obviously far more primitive than anything we would recognize today.

The financial model underpinning all of this activity rested on a combination of sources that shifted in relative importance across Roman history. In the earliest periods, individual magistrates sponsoring games, a practice tied to religious festivals and increasingly to political self promotion during the late Republic, would contract directly with faction owners to supply horses, chariots, and drivers for a specific set of races, paying a fee that covered the faction's costs and, if negotiated well, left a healthy profit margin. This arrangement gave ambitious Roman politicians a direct incentive to fund increasingly lavish games as a form of public relations, since a spectacular set of races, remembered fondly by the voting public, could translate directly into political support at election time. Julius Caesar, among many other

Roman politicians of the late Republic, was noted by ancient biographers for spending enormous personal sums on public games during his early career specifically to build popular support, well before he held the kind of formal power that would later let him fund such spectacles from the public treasury directly.

As the Republic gave way to the Empire, and as emperors increasingly took over direct responsibility for funding major public games, the financial relationship between the state and the racing factions became more formalized and, in some respects, more secure for the factions themselves. Imperial subsidy, once established as a regular practice, gave faction owners a predictable revenue stream that reduced their exposure to the uncertainty of relying on individual magistrates who might or might not choose to fund elaborate games in any given year. This shift toward stable, state backed funding likely contributed to the increasing scale and professionalization of the factions across the first and second centuries, since predictable revenue allows for exactly the kind of long term investment, in breeding programs, in staff training, in physical infrastructure, that short term contract work discourages. A faction owner confident of receiving regular imperial commissions could invest in a multi year horse breeding program with far more confidence than one dependent on the unpredictable generosity of individual sponsoring magistrates.

Prize money constituted a second major revenue stream, though its distribution reveals a great deal about the internal economics of a faction that is easy to overlook if one focuses only on famous charioteers like Diocles, whose personal earnings this book will examine in detail in a later chapter. When a charioteer won a race, the prize money did not simply become his personal property in the way that, say, a modern tennis player keeps their tournament winnings outright. Ancient evidence, while incomplete on the precise contractual terms involved, strongly suggests that faction owners retained a substantial share of race winnings, using this revenue to cover the faction's enormous ongoing operating costs: horse feed, staff wages, equipment, veterinary care, and the constant need to acquire new horses and train new drivers to replace those lost to injury, death, or the natural attrition of a physically brutal sport. The charioteer himself received a portion, and for the most successful drivers this portion could still amount to a genuine fortune, but it is important to understand the faction, not the individual driver, as the primary economic unit generating and retaining wealth from the sport. This is closer to a modern professional sports franchise model, in which individual athletes are paid substantial sums but the organization itself retains and reinvests the majority of overall revenue, than to a purely individual entrepreneurial model in which each competitor operates as an independent economic agent.

A third and more socially fraught revenue category involved private betting, though here the historical record grows considerably murkier and requires careful handling. Roman sources are unambiguous that private wagering on chariot races was widespread and often intense, cutting across every level of society from enslaved spectators wagering small sums to senators and, on documented occasions, emperors themselves placing substantial bets. What remains genuinely unclear, and here honest historical caution matters more than narrative convenience, is whether the racing factions themselves operated any form of official bookmaking or simply benefited indirectly from the general excitement and attendance that widespread betting generated. There is no clear evidence of a formalized, faction operated betting apparatus comparable to a modern sportsbook. What existed instead appears to have been a decentralized, essentially private betting culture, conducted between individual spectators or through informal intermediaries, that the factions did not directly control but from which they benefited enormously in terms of heightened public engagement, larger crowds, and the intensified emotional investment that turned casual spectators into devoted, lifelong fans. This distinction matters for anyone trying to reconstruct an accurate picture of faction finances, and this book will return to the betting economy in far greater detail in a later chapter dedicated specifically to that subject, including the physical evidence, curse tablets buried at the Circus by fans hoping to sabotage rival teams, that gives us our clearest window into just how much money and emotion rode on individual races.

The rivalry between the four factions was not, it is worth emphasizing, a matter of gentle sporting competition conducted with polite mutual respect. Ancient sources describe faction loyalty as something closer to a total social identity, comparable in intensity to modern political party affiliation or, in some documented instances of urban violence, to something considerably more volatile than anything most modern sports fandoms would recognize. This intensity had direct economic consequences, because it meant that a faction's on track success translated almost immediately into increased public attention, increased attendance at races specifically to see that faction compete, and, very plausibly, increased informal betting activity concentrated around whichever faction currently held public favor. A successful faction was not merely a well run business in a narrow operational sense. It was, in effect, a popular brand, commanding the kind of public loyalty that modern marketing executives spend enormous sums trying to manufacture and that the Roman factions appear to have generated organically, or at least with far less deliberate promotional effort, simply through sustained on track success and colorful, larger than life driver personalities.

Archaeological investigation of Rome itself has helped confirm the physical scale of these faction operations described in ancient legal and literary sources. Remains associated with faction stable complexes, located in the districts surrounding the Circus Maximus and in the Campus Martius area of the city, reveal substantial purpose built structures rather than improvised or temporary facilities, further evidence that the four factions operated as permanent, capital intensive institutions rather than seasonal or occasional commercial ventures assembled anew before each race day. These stable complexes needed to accommodate not only the horses themselves but the extensive staff this chapter has already documented, along with storage for equipment, chariots, and the substantial quantities of feed that sustaining a large population of competition horses required on a daily, year round basis. The physical footprint of a major faction's Roman operations, in other words, extended well beyond the Circus Maximus itself into a broader network of supporting facilities scattered across the city, a detail that reinforces this chapter's broader argument that the four colors of Roman chariot racing represented substantial, permanent commercial institutions fully integrated into the physical and economic fabric of the city, rather than a loosely organized set of arrangements convened only when race day approached.

By the second century of the common era, the Blue and Green factions had emerged as the dominant forces in the sport, gradually absorbing much of the talent, resources, and public attention that had once been more evenly distributed across all four colors. The Red and White factions did not disappear entirely, and charioteers continued to race under all four colors well into Late Antiquity, but the concentration of resources and prestige into two dominant factions foreshadows a pattern familiar to any observer of modern commercial competition: an industry that begins with several roughly comparable competitors tends, over time, to consolidate around a smaller number of dominant players who can outspend and outperform their rivals, absorbing market share until only a duopoly, or something close to it, remains standing. This consolidation would become even more pronounced by the time the sport's center of gravity shifted eastward to Constantinople in Late Antiquity, a development this book examines closely in a later chapter devoted to the charioteer Porphyrius and the

Byzantine hippodrome economy that grew directly out of the Roman model described here.

What should be clear by the end of this chapter, and what the remainder of this book will continue to demonstrate in ever greater detail, is that the four colors of Roman chariot racing were never simply decorative team affiliations in the way a modern reader might casually assume. They were the branding of four substantial, highly capitalized commercial enterprises, each managing complex logistics networks, substantial workforces, significant fixed and variable costs, and revenue streams drawn from public subsidy, prize competition, and the indirect commercial benefits of intense, sustained popular loyalty. The domini factionum who ran these operations were businessmen first and sporting patrons second, however much later romantic tradition has preferred to remember them purely in terms of colorful rivalry and dramatic races. Before we can follow a single charioteer onto the sand of the Circus Maximus, we needed to understand the corporate structure that put him there, fed and trained the horses pulling his chariot, and stood to profit, far more than he ever would personally, from every victory he achieved. The next chapter turns to the animals themselves, and to a breeding and trading economy that stretched across three continents in service of four colors and one enormous appetite for speed.

CHAPTER THREE

BREEDING FORTUNES

What made a horse worth a fortune in the ancient world, and who decided which animals were destined for glory and which for the plow?

The Roman agricultural writer Columella, composing his twelve volume treatise on farming sometime in the middle of the first century, took the question seriously enough to devote careful attention to it in his sixth book, which deals with the raising and management of livestock. Columella divided horses into three distinct categories, a classification system that tells us a great deal about how systematically the Romans thought about equine breeding as an economic activity rather than a matter of chance or tradition. The first category, which he called generosa materies, the noble stock, consisted of horses bred specifically for competition in the circus and at the sacred games. The second category comprised horses bred for producing mules, an activity Columella notes commanded prices comparable to the noble racing stock itself, a detail that should immediately signal to a modern reader just how commercially significant equine breeding was as an industry in its own right, entirely apart from its connection to spectator entertainment. The third and lowest category was simply common stock, animals bred for ordinary riding and transport without any pretense of exceptional quality.

This tripartite classification was not an abstract taxonomic exercise. It reflected an entire economic infrastructure built around identifying, breeding, and training horses for the specific and extraordinarily demanding purpose of circus competition, and it represented centuries of accumulated practical knowledge about which bloodlines, which regions, and which training regimens produced animals capable of surviving, let alone winning, races that pushed both horse and driver to genuine physical extremity. The stakes involved in getting this right were substantial. A faction that consistently fielded superior horses held an enormous competitive advantage over rivals fielding merely adequate stock, and the financial rewards of victory, in prize money, in public prestige, and in the ongoing subsidy that a successful faction could command from wealthy patrons and eventually from the imperial treasury itself, made the identification and acquisition of quality breeding stock one of the single most consequential business decisions a faction owner or his agents could make.

Certain regions of the Roman world developed reputations, well attested across multiple ancient sources spanning several centuries, as premier suppliers of circus quality horses. Hispania, the

Iberian peninsula encompassing modern Spain and Portugal, stood at the top of this list, its horses prized for a combination of speed, stamina, and a temperament suited to the punishing demands of chariot competition. North Africa, particularly the region the Romans associated with Barbary stock, contributed horses celebrated for their heat tolerance, quickness, and hardiness, qualities that made them especially valued in an environment where a race might be run under the full heat of a Roman summer afternoon in front of a crowd numbering in the hundreds of thousands. Cappadocia, in the highlands of central Anatolia, rounded out what ancient writers generally treated as the three most significant sources of quality circus stock, though additional breeding centers in Greece, Sicily, and southern Italy also supplied horses to the industry, particularly for factions and amateur owners operating with smaller budgets than the great Roman stables could command.

The geographic spread of these breeding centers deserves a moment of genuine appreciation, because it illustrates something important about the scale and sophistication of the ancient economy that supported chariot racing. A faction owner in Rome seeking to acquire top tier breeding stock was not simply purchasing animals from a local market. He was, in effect, operating an international procurement network stretching from the Atlantic coast of Iberia through North

Africa to the highlands of Anatolia, a geographic range spanning thousands of miles that required reliable maritime transport, trustworthy agents capable of evaluating horseflesh on the ground in distant provinces, and sufficient capital to make substantial purchases, arrange transportation, and absorb the very real risk of losing valuable animals to disease, injury, or the simple hazards of sea travel before they ever reached Rome. This was commercial activity conducted at a genuinely impressive scale and level of sophistication for a preindustrial economy, one that depended on functioning maritime trade routes, a reasonably reliable system of long distance communication and credit, and a shared commercial culture, spanning the length of the Mediterranean, in which buyers and sellers separated by enormous distances could conduct business with some confidence that contracts would be honored and goods delivered as promised.

Training a horse for circus competition began well before the animal ever set hoof on the track at the Circus Maximus. Ancient sources indicate that serious training commenced when a horse reached roughly three years of age, with animals typically not entering actual competition until they reached five, a two year developmental period during which trainers assessed temperament, built physical conditioning, and began the specialized work of teaching a horse to respond to the specific demands of circus racing, an activity that bears only partial resemblance to ordinary riding or draft work. Circus racing required a horse to accept being harnessed alongside three other animals in a four horse team, called a quadriga, coordinating its movement and pace with teammates it had not necessarily grown up alongside, tolerating the deafening roar of a crowd that could exceed a hundred thousand voices, and executing tight, high speed turns around the metae, the turning posts at either end of the central spina, where the greatest risk of catastrophic collision and injury occurred. This was a highly specialized athletic discipline, and the training regimen developed to prepare horses for it reflected genuine expertise refined across many generations of practical experience.

Not every horse in a four horse team performed the same role, a detail that further illustrates the sophistication of Roman equine management. Ancient evidence indicates that the two inner horses, harnessed directly to the chariot pole, were typically selected for strength and steadiness, since these animals bore the primary burden of pulling the vehicle and maintaining a controlled pace through the straights. The outer horses, particularly the horse on the left side nearest the spina during the tight turns around the metae, required exceptional agility and responsiveness, since this animal effectively pivoted the entire team through the turn and bore disproportionate responsibility for both the speed and the safety of the maneuver. A faction seeking to assemble a truly elite racing team was not simply acquiring four fast horses. It was assembling a coordinated athletic unit in which different animals filled genuinely different functional roles, each requiring somewhat different physical and temperamental qualities, a level of tactical sophistication that modern readers, accustomed to thinking of ancient sport as comparatively primitive, may find genuinely surprising.

The financial value attached to exceptional circus horses is difficult to pin down with the kind of precision a modern economic historian would prefer, since the Roman world left behind no equivalent of a modern auction house sale record or standardized market price index. What we do have are scattered but suggestive pieces of evidence that, taken together, paint a picture of an industry in which truly outstanding horses commanded prices that placed them among the most valuable movable property a wealthy Roman might own. Individual horses achieved genuine fame in their own right, celebrated by name in poetry, commemorated on mosaics found throughout the Roman world from Britain to North Africa, and mourned in verse when they died, a level of individual recognition and emotional investment that stands in sharp contrast to the largely anonymous treatment of ordinary livestock in Roman agricultural writing. Martial, the first century epigrammatist whose short, often satirical poems provide some of our richest surviving evidence of everyday Roman cultural attitudes, referenced famous circus horses by name with the casual familiarity of a modern sports writer mentioning a celebrated athlete, evidence that these animals had achieved a level of public recognition and, implicitly, economic value that ordinary farm horses never approached.

The mosaic evidence deserves particular attention here, because it offers some of our most vivid surviving testimony to the individual celebrity that top circus horses achieved. Multiple mosaics recovered from Roman sites across North Africa, a region with a particularly strong tradition of circus themed decorative art, depict named horses alongside named charioteers, treating the animals as full partners in athletic achievement rather than merely as equipment or property. A mosaic from Hadrumetum, in what is now Tunisia, portrays four charioteers representing all four factions together with their horses, each animal individually identified, a level of specific commemoration that would be genuinely unusual for ordinary livestock in almost any other context in the ancient world. This pattern repeats across multiple archaeological sites, suggesting that the practice of celebrating individual circus horses by name was a widespread and culturally significant phenomenon rather than an isolated curiosity, and it provides indirect but compelling evidence that the animals themselves represented substantial economic and cultural capital, not merely interchangeable components of a larger racing apparatus.

Beyond the breeding and training operations directly controlled or contracted by the four major factions, ancient evidence also points to a broader amateur and semi professional layer of horse ownership and racing participation that operated somewhat outside the main commercial structure this book has described so far. Individual wealthy Romans and, notably, entire municipalities in the provinces sometimes owned and fielded their own racing teams, participating in exhibition events that ran alongside the main professional faction competitions. This was, by all accounts, an expensive undertaking, one available only to individuals or civic bodies with substantial disposable wealth, but it created an additional layer of demand for quality breeding stock beyond what the four major Roman factions alone required, further expanding the market for the specialized breeding operations described earlier in this chapter and helping to explain why breeding centers as geographically dispersed as Cappadocia, Sicily, and southern Italy could all sustain commercially viable operations supplying circus quality horses to a market considerably larger than the needs of the four dominant factions in Rome alone.

The ongoing cost of simply maintaining a competitive racing stable, once the initial acquisition of quality breeding stock had been accomplished, deserves separate consideration, since it represented a substantial and continuous drain on faction resources entirely apart from the upfront purchase price of the animals themselves. A circus horse in active training or competition required a diet considerably richer and more carefully managed than the ordinary grazing sufficient for ordinary draft or agricultural animals, and ancient veterinary writers, a genre of technical literature that developed specifically to serve the needs of exactly this kind of specialized, high value animal husbandry, describe feeding regimens involving grain supplements considerably more expensive than simple pasture grass. Multiply this ongoing feed cost across the substantial number of horses, modern estimates drawing on the logistics of a full day's racing program suggest as many as seven or eight hundred horses might be required to stage a complete schedule of races at a major venue, that a faction needed to maintain in various stages of training, competition readiness, and retirement at any given time, and the aggregate ongoing operating expense of a major Roman racing stable begins to look less like the cost of a hobby and considerably more like the sustained capital intensive operating budget of a substantial ancient commercial enterprise, comparable in scale and complexity to the largest agricultural estates or mining operations that Roman economic historians study using more conventional categories of ancient business activity.

It is worth pausing to consider what all of this meant for the individuals actually engaged in the breeding and training work itself, a population that has left far fainter traces in the historical record than the famous charioteers and their celebrated horses, but whose labor was absolutely essential to the entire economic edifice this book is describing. Breeding farms required skilled staff capable of managing complex animal husbandry operations across multiple years, from selecting appropriate breeding pairs through to the extended training process that transformed a promising young horse into a genuine competitor. Much of this labor, like much of the labor throughout the Roman economy generally, was performed by enslaved individuals, working alongside a smaller number of free specialists who brought particular expertise in veterinary care or advanced training techniques. The economic value generated by a successful breeding operation, in other words, rested substantially on enslaved labor, a pattern that recurs throughout this book's examination of the chariot racing industry and that will receive fuller and more direct treatment in the following chapter, which turns from the horses themselves to the human beings, many of them enslaved at the outset of their careers, who drove them.

The picture that emerges from even this necessarily incomplete survey of Roman circus horse breeding is one of a genuinely sophisticated commercial agricultural sector, organized around specialized regional production centers, systematic classification of breeding stock by intended use, a demanding multi year training regimen grounded in accumulated practical expertise about equine athletic performance, and a market sustaining prices for exceptional animals that placed them among the most valuable forms of movable property available in the ancient Mediterranean world. This was not a peripheral or incidental economic activity conducted as an afterthought to the more celebrated business of the racing factions themselves. It was a foundational industry in its own right, one that stretched from the highland pastures of Cappadocia to the North African plains to the river valleys of Hispania, moving valuable animals across the length of the Mediterranean world in service of an entertainment industry with an apparently insatiable appetite for the next great champion. The men and, in the case of the enslaved labor force, the men and women who bred, trained, and transported these animals rarely appear by name in the surviving historical record, but the scale and sophistication of the industry they sustained speaks clearly enough for itself. Before a single chariot ever crossed the starting line at the Circus Maximus, an entire economy of breeding farms, sea captains, veterinary specialists, and provincial agents had already done the essential work of producing the animals without which the entire spectacle, and the entire financial empire built upon it, simply could not have existed.

The next chapter turns from the horses to the men who drove them, tracing the remarkable and often brutal career path that could carry an enslaved boy from complete anonymity to a level of wealth and public celebrity that few free born Romans of any social class ever achieved.

CHAPTER FOUR

SLAVES WHO BECAME MILLIONAIRES

Picture a boy, perhaps eight or nine years old, purchased by a faction agent in a slave market somewhere in the Roman provinces. He has no name that history will remember, no family the record keeps track of, and no reason to expect that his life will be different from the thousands of other enslaved children absorbed into the vast and largely anonymous labor force that powered the Roman economy. And yet, for a small number of boys who found themselves in exactly this position, the path that opened before them led somewhere almost nobody else born into slavery in the ancient world could realistically hope to reach: genuine fortune, public celebrity on a scale rivaling senators and emperors, and eventual freedom purchased not through the slow accumulation of a domestic servant's modest savings, but through winnings that could, in the most extraordinary cases, exceed the wealth of entire aristocratic families.

This chapter tells the story of that path, from purchase to training to competition to, for the fortunate few, freedom and fortune, and it does so without flinching from the brutal reality that sat underneath even the most spectacular success stories. The Roman chariot racing industry offered one of the very few routes by which an enslaved person in the ancient world might climb, through sheer individual skill and no small amount of luck, into genuine wealth. That this route existed at all says something remarkable about the peculiar economics of celebrity spectacle in the Roman world. That it existed within a system built fundamentally on the ownership and exploitation of human beings should never be forgotten or softened for the sake of a tidier narrative.

The Roman charioteer, known generically in Latin as an auriga or agitator, entered the profession almost exclusively as a young slave purchased and trained by one of the four major racing factions. Modern statistical analysis of surviving charioteer epitaphs and commemorative inscriptions, drawing on a body of more than two hundred documented individuals compiled by historians working through the epigraphic record, indicates that the overwhelming majority of identifiable charioteers began their careers enslaved. Free born participation in professional chariot racing was, by contrast, exceptionally rare, attested in only a handful of documented cases across the entire span of the sport's history. This was, in other words, overwhelmingly an occupation staffed through the institution of slavery, and the factions approached the acquisition and training of young charioteers with the same systematic commercial logic they applied to the acquisition and training of racing horses described in the previous chapter. A faction seeking to remain competitive needed a continuous pipeline of new talent, since the sport's brutal physical demands guaranteed a constant attrition of drivers through injury, death, and the simple wearing effects of age on a body pushed to its limits race after race for years on end.

Roman terminology distinguished between two ranks within the profession, and understanding this distinction illuminates the career trajectory a successful charioteer might follow. The term auriga, in its narrower technical sense, referred to a less experienced driver typically assigned to the biga, the lighter two horse chariot used in preliminary or lower stakes events. As a driver demonstrated skill and survived long enough to accumulate genuine experience, he might advance to the rank of agitator, the accomplished driver entrusted with the quadriga, the standard four horse team, and in the case of the most celebrated competitors, with even larger and more difficult teams of six, eight, or in rare and highly celebrated instances, as many as ten horses. This progression from auriga to agitator represented both an increase in status and, crucially for the purposes of this book, a dramatic increase in earning potential, since the major races commanding the largest prize purses were reserved for the quadriga competitions and their still more demanding multi horse variants, events in which only the most skilled and experienced drivers competed.

The physical dangers involved in this profession were not incidental risks tolerated as an unfortunate byproduct of an otherwise glamorous occupation. They were central and unavoidable features of the job, and the Romans themselves designed the equipment of chariot racing with a grim, practical acknowledgment of just how frequently things went catastrophically wrong. Unlike a modern image of a driver holding loose reins in his hands, ready to release them at the first sign of trouble, the Roman charioteer wrapped the reins tightly around his waist, using his entire body weight to control and steer the team through the tremendous forces generated at racing speed. This method offered the driver far greater control and leverage over a team of powerful horses than his hands alone could provide, but it came at a horrifying cost in the event of a crash. A charioteer thrown from his vehicle, or dragged from it in a collision, remained bound to his horses by the reins wrapped around his own body, and could be dragged across the sand at lethal speed, trampled by his own team or by the teams of competitors racing close behind. For precisely this reason, every charioteer carried a curved knife called a falx tucked into his belt, a tool with exactly one grim purpose: to cut himself free from the reins in the desperate seconds after a crash, before being dragged to death. That the Romans equipped every single charioteer with a device specifically designed to save his life in the aftermath of an accident tells us, more clearly than any narrative account could, just how routinely such accidents occurred. This was not an occasional hazard. It was an expected and recurring feature of the profession, one that shortened careers and ended lives with grim regularity, and it is impossible to understand the financial rewards available to successful charioteers without also understanding the mortal risk that made those rewards, in a very real sense, a form of hazard pay for one of the most dangerous professions in the ancient world.

Before a young enslaved boy ever approached the starting gate in genuine competition, he passed through an extended apprenticeship that mirrored, in its structured, multi year progression, the horse training regimen this book's third chapter described in detail. A newly acquired charioteer in training began with basic work around the stables themselves, tending horses, learning the equipment, and absorbing the accumulated practical knowledge of more experienced drivers and trainers before ever taking the reins in anything resembling a real competitive setting. Progression to actual driving typically began with the lighter, less demanding biga, the two horse chariot, in minor or exhibition events where the stakes, both financial and physical, were considerably lower than the major quadriga races that would eventually define a successful driver's reputation and earnings. Only after demonstrating genuine competence and, crucially, surviving this initial period without catastrophic injury, would a faction entrust its more valuable four horse teams and its larger financial commitments to a given young driver, a gradual escalation of responsibility that reflects the same careful, capital conscious risk management this book has identified as a defining feature of how factions approached every other aspect of their commercial operations, from horse breeding through prize money allocation. This apprenticeship structure meant that the population of young charioteers entering the profession at any given time considerably exceeded the number who ultimately achieved the kind of sustained, lucrative careers this chapter and the next examine in detail, with an unknown but almost certainly substantial number of young trainees failing to progress beyond the earliest, lowest stakes phases of competition, their subsequent fates largely invisible to the historical record that preserves, disproportionately, the names and achievements of the profession's most spectacular successes.

Given these risks, why would any faction, or any enslaved individual forced into this occupation, continue investing in it generation after generation? The answer lies in the financial incentives on both sides of the relationship, incentives that, however unsettling to modern sensibilities when applied to a system of human bondage, functioned with genuine internal economic logic. For the faction, a successful charioteer represented an enormously valuable asset, one whose victories generated prize money, enhanced the faction's public reputation and fan loyalty, and, in the case of truly exceptional drivers, attracted the kind of celebrity attention that could translate into increased patronage and public subsidy for the faction as a whole. Investing years of training and support in a promising young driver was, from the faction's perspective, a calculated capital investment not fundamentally different from the extended breeding and training programs the faction maintained for its horses, and the very best charioteers repaid this investment many times over across careers that, for the fortunate and skilled, could stretch across two or even three decades.

For the enslaved individual himself, the incentive structure, however coercive its ultimate origins, created a genuine and highly unusual pathway toward the accumulation of personal wealth, a pathway essentially unavailable to almost any other category of enslaved labor in the Roman world. Historians studying the epigraphic record of charioteer careers have found that successful drivers were typically manumitted, formally freed from slavery, around the age of thirty, a pattern suggesting that faction owners recognized a functioning economic bargain in which years of successful racing earned a driver his eventual freedom, often financed in substantial part by the driver's own accumulated winnings. This was manumission achieved not through the patient, decades long domestic service that characterized the path to freedom for most enslaved Romans, but through direct athletic achievement and the prize money that achievement generated, a route to liberty tied explicitly to individual performance in a way that had few parallels elsewhere in Roman slavery. Roman law recognized several formal mechanisms for manumission, including manumissio vindicta, a formal ceremony conducted before a magistrate, and it is entirely plausible, though the specific documentary evidence for any individual charioteer's manumission proceedings rarely survives in full detail, that successful drivers pursued these established legal channels once they had accumulated sufficient winnings and standing to negotiate their freedom with their faction owners.

Once freed, a former slave charioteer entered Roman society as a libertus, a freedman, a legal and social status that carried its own complicated mixture of opportunity and continued limitation. Freedmen gained Roman citizenship, or a limited form of it depending on the specific circumstances of their manumission, and could legally own property, enter into contracts, and, crucially for a wealthy former charioteer, invest and manage substantial personal fortunes. Yet freedmen remained permanently marked by their former servile status in the eyes of much of Roman society, barred from certain political offices and social positions reserved for the freeborn, and subject to lingering social prejudice regardless of how much wealth they accumulated. Historians studying Roman charioteers have also noted the legal category of infamia, a formal diminishment of civil standing that Roman law applied to individuals engaged in certain professions considered disreputable despite their public popularity, a category that some scholars believe applied to at least some charioteers, though the precise scope and consistency of this legal disability across the entire history of the profession remains a subject of genuine scholarly debate rather than settled certainty. This is one of the many places where this book must acknowledge honest uncertainty in the historical record rather than manufacturing false confidence: we know that successful charioteers achieved wealth and public adoration on a scale that dwarfed most other paths available to former slaves, and we also know that Roman society never fully extended to them the unambiguous social respectability that their wealth alone might seem to warrant in a purely economic reading of their position.

The financial rewards available to the most successful charioteers are worth dwelling on in concrete terms, because the figures involved genuinely strain modern intuition about what an ancient economy could support. A single day's prize earnings for a top charioteer, according to comparisons made by historians working from surviving evidence, could exceed the entire annual salary of a Roman schoolteacher, a comparison that captures just how dramatically the economics of celebrity spectacle diverged from the economics of ordinary skilled labor in the ancient world. The following chapter of this book will examine in granular, race by race detail the career of Gaius Appuleius Diocles, whose surviving inscription provides our single richest source of hard financial data about charioteer earnings anywhere in the ancient world, and whose total career winnings, an almost incomprehensible thirty five million, eight hundred sixty three thousand, one hundred twenty sesterces accumulated across twenty four years of racing, place him among the most extraordinary individual financial success stories to survive from Roman antiquity in any profession, free or enslaved. But Diocles, however exceptional, was not entirely alone. Ancient sources reference numerous other charioteers who achieved substantial fame and fortune, including drivers like

Pompeius Musclosus, who according to surviving records accumulated an even greater total number of individual victories than Diocles across his own career, even if his total prize winnings did not reach quite the same staggering financial heights, since Diocles proved especially adept at winning the largest, highest value races rather than simply accumulating victories across events of every size.

What emerges from this examination is a labor market unlike almost anything else in the ancient Mediterranean economy: one in which enslaved status at the point of entry was nearly universal, in which the physical risks of the occupation were severe and routinely fatal, and in which the financial and social rewards available to the small fraction of participants who achieved genuine success were so extraordinary that they inverted, at least for a handful of individuals, the normal economic relationship between free and enslaved persons in Roman society. A successful charioteer, freed in his early thirties with a fortune built from two decades of prize winnings, might well have commanded greater personal wealth than the vast majority of freeborn Roman citizens he would encounter for the remainder of his life, even as those same citizens continued to regard him, on account of his origins and his profession, as someone whose social standing remained permanently compromised. This tension, between extraordinary individual economic achievement and persistent social limitation, runs throughout the history of Roman chariot racing and offers a genuinely striking parallel to debates that continue in modern professional sports about the relationship between athletic wealth, fame, and full social acceptance, a parallel this book will return to more directly in its concluding chapters.

The next chapter turns fully to Diocles himself, examining in detail the remarkable inscription that preserves his career statistics with a level of granularity almost unmatched anywhere else in the surviving record of ancient sport, and using that single, extraordinarily rich document as a window into exactly how the financial machinery described across these opening chapters, the factions, the breeding networks, and the labor market for charioteers, actually operated in the career of one specific, documented human being.

CHAPTER FIVE

THE DIOCLES LEDGER

"Gaius Appuleius Diocles, charioteer of the Red stable, a Lusitanian Spaniard by birth, aged forty two years, seven months, and twenty three days."

So begins one of the most extraordinary documents to survive from the entire span of Roman antiquity, a monumental inscription erected in the year 146 of the common era, commissioned, it appears, by the man it commemorates while he was still very much alive to enjoy the recognition. Catalogued by modern scholars as CIL VI, number 10048, part of the great compendium of Latin inscriptions assembled from across the former Roman world, this single stone monument provides a level of granular, quantified detail about one individual's professional career that has no real parallel anywhere else in surviving ancient literature or epigraphy, athletic or otherwise. We do not possess anything comparable for a Roman senator, a celebrated general, or an emperor. We possess it for a charioteer, a man born into a Roman province who began his working life, in all likelihood, enslaved, and this chapter is devoted entirely to unpacking exactly what that inscription tells us, and what it means for our understanding of the financial machinery this book has been describing.

Diocles began racing at the age of eighteen, in the year 122, competing initially for the White faction, the color under which most young charioteers, following the standard career pattern this book described in the previous chapter, entered professional competition. After six years driving for the Whites, he moved to the Greens, a faction with whom, according to the inscription's own account, he experienced a comparatively difficult period, including what the monument describes in terms suggesting some form of injury or setback that affected his performance during this phase of his career. It was only when Diocles moved to the Red faction, where he would remain for the following fifteen years and complete the majority of his most celebrated victories, that his career reached its full extraordinary heights. This trajectory across three of the four major factions is itself worth pausing on, because it illustrates something important about the labor market for elite charioteers that this book has not yet fully addressed: the most talented drivers were not necessarily bound permanently to a single faction for the whole of their careers. Diocles moved between factions multiple times, a pattern that strongly suggests a competitive market for proven talent, in which successful charioteers, or the faction owners who effectively controlled their careers, could negotiate moves in pursuit of better terms, stronger supporting teams of horses, or simply a better fit with a faction's particular racing strategy and management.

The raw statistics recorded on the monument are worth setting out in full, because their sheer scale is essential to appreciating exactly what kind of career this document describes. Over twenty four years of competition, Diocles started in four thousand two hundred fifty seven races. He won one thousand four hundred sixty two of them outright, a winning percentage of roughly thirty four percent, a figure that, for a sport in which every single race involved intense competition against the empire's other most skilled drivers, represents a truly extraordinary level of sustained excellence across nearly two and a half decades of competition. The inscription breaks these victories down with a precision that borders on the obsessive: one thousand sixty four of his wins came in single entry races, the standard format pitting one chariot per faction against the others. Ninety two of his victories came in what the inscription describes as major prizes, high value races carrying especially large purses, and of these ninety two major victories, the monument specifies the exact purse amount for each category: thirty two victories worth thirty thousand sesterces each, twenty eight worth forty thousand sesterces each, twenty nine worth fifty thousand sesterces each, and three worth sixty thousand sesterces each, figures that included several races driven with the more difficult six and seven horse teams that only the most accomplished charioteers ever attempted.

Beyond simple victory counts, the inscription records Diocles' tactical patterns with a specificity that gives us a genuinely rare window into the actual racing strategy employed by an elite ancient charioteer. He won eight hundred fifteen times by leading from the starting gate and maintaining that lead throughout the race, a straightforward front running strategy. He won sixty seven times coming from behind, presumably holding back in the early laps before making a decisive late move, a tactic that later sources describing his career specifically praise as his signature approach, and that likely explains why he could compete effectively against faster but less tactically patient rivals. He won thirty six times after being passed at some point during the race and then recovering to reclaim the lead, and five hundred two times specifically at the finish line itself, presumably in close, contested races decided in the race's final meters. This level of tactical granularity, preserved for a single individual across a career spanning more than four thousand documented starts, is simply unmatched anywhere else in the surviving record of ancient athletic competition, and it allows modern readers a startlingly intimate view into exactly how one of history's most successful competitive drivers actually approached his craft.

The monument also records Diocles' record against each of the rival factions individually: two hundred sixteen victories against the Greens, two hundred five against the Blues, and eighty one against the Whites, the faction with whom he began his own career. It notes that nine of his horses achieved one hundred career victories driving with Diocles, and remarkably, that a single horse achieved two hundred victories partnered with him, a detail that underscores the point made in the previous chapter about the genuine individual celebrity that exceptional circus horses achieved in their own right, celebrated by name and by career record with a specificity that rivaled the recognition given to their human drivers.

And then there is the figure that has made Diocles a subject of fascination well beyond the narrow circle of specialists in Roman social and economic history: his total career winnings, recorded on the monument as thirty five million, eight hundred sixty three thousand, one hundred twenty sesterces. Modern historians attempting to translate this figure into terms a contemporary reader can meaningfully grasp have approached the problem from several different angles, each with its own limitations, since converting ancient currency values into modern equivalents is an inherently imprecise exercise given the vastly different structure of the ancient and modern economies. One frequently cited comparison, developed by Peter Struck, a classical studies scholar at the University of Pennsylvania, calculated that Diocles' total winnings would have been sufficient to provide grain for the entire population of the city of Rome for a full year, or alternatively, to fund the Roman army at the height of its imperial power for a period exceeding two months. Struck extended this comparison into a rough modern dollar estimate, suggesting a figure in the neighborhood of fifteen billion dollars when measured against the cost of sustaining a comparably sized modern military force for an equivalent period, a calculation that, whatever one thinks of its precise methodology, communicates the essential point with real force: Diocles' documented earnings placed him in a category of individual wealth that modern professional athletes, for all the genuine riches available in contemporary sport, have only recently begun to approach, and that stood as a genuinely staggering sum by the standards of his own society regardless of how one chooses to convert it into present day terms.

The physical monument itself deserves a brief description, since its form tells us something about how Diocles and his contemporaries understood the significance of what was being recorded. The inscription survives as a substantial carved stone monument, the kind of formal commemorative object that wealthy and socially prominent Romans commissioned to mark significant life achievements, funerary monuments, dedications to the gods, records of public service and civic benefaction. That a charioteer, a man who began his working life enslaved, could commission and erect a monument of this scale and formality, employing skilled stone carvers to render his career statistics in the same durable medium and with the same evident expectation of permanence that a senator might use to record his own political and military accomplishments, is itself a remarkable statement about the social and economic position successful charioteers had come to occupy within Roman society by the second century. The monument does not survive complete in its original context, and modern scholars studying it, working from the text preserved in the great compendium of Latin inscriptions, have had to reconstruct its likely original form and setting from the surviving textual content and comparison with similar commemorative monuments from the period. What is clear from the surviving text alone is that Diocles, or those close to him who assisted in commissioning the monument, approached the task of recording his career with the same careful, comprehensive attention to detail that a modern professional archivist might bring to compiling a definitive statistical record, an approach to self commemoration that stands in genuinely striking contrast to the far vaguer and more impressionistic language Roman funerary inscriptions typically employ when describing the achievements of even quite wealthy and prominent individuals from other walks of Roman life.

It is worth pausing here for a moment of genuine methodological honesty, since this book has promised throughout to distinguish clearly between solid documentary evidence and necessary but more speculative interpretation. The figure of 35,863,120 sesterces is not itself in dispute. It is carved in stone, in a monument that Diocles himself, by all indications, commissioned and approved during his own lifetime, giving him every incentive to ensure the figures were, from his own perspective and by whatever accounting method the factions used internally, accurate. What remains genuinely uncertain, and what any responsible historian must acknowledge rather than paper over, is precisely how this gross figure relates to Diocles' actual personal wealth after the faction's own substantial share, described in the previous chapter, was deducted from race winnings before any portion reached the driver himself. The inscription records what Diocles won, or what was credited to him and his faction jointly, across his racing career. It does not provide us with anything resembling a personal balance sheet showing his net accumulated wealth after decades of the faction's operating costs, his own living expenses, and whatever portion of his winnings he may have used to purchase his own eventual freedom had been subtracted from the gross totals so carefully recorded on his monument. Any modern attempt to state with confidence exactly how personally wealthy Diocles became, expressed as a precise dollar figure, is engaging in a degree of extrapolation considerably beyond what the primary evidence alone can strictly support, however useful such comparisons are for conveying the general scale of what this single career achieved.

What we can say with confidence, resting directly on the inscription's own carefully recorded figures, is that Diocles represents documented proof of something this entire book has been arguing from its opening pages: that Roman chariot racing generated and moved genuinely enormous sums of money, concentrated in this instance in the recorded career of a single driver whose own account of his earnings, inscribed in stone for future generations to read, shows a financial scale that would not become common in professional athletics again until the modern era of televised, globally broadcast sport, nearly two thousand years later. The specificity of the inscription, its willingness to break down earnings by exact purse category, by tactical victory type, by opposing faction, and by individual horse, also tells us something important about the culture that produced it. This was not a society embarrassed by or indifferent to precise financial accounting in the context of celebrity athletic achievement. It was a society that valued exactly this kind of quantified detail enough to carve it permanently in stone, suggesting that Diocles' contemporary audience, the Roman public who would have read or heard this monument's inscription, possessed both the numerical literacy and the cultural appetite to appreciate figures presented with this degree of granular precision, much as a modern sports audience consumes and discusses detailed statistical records of contemporary athletes with genuine enthusiasm.

Diocles retired in the year 146, at the age of forty two, having spent twenty four years in a profession that, as the previous chapter detailed, killed a great many of its practitioners well before they reached anything resembling old age by ancient standards. That he survived to retire at all placed him among a fortunate minority of successful long term charioteers. That he retired with a documented fortune of this scale placed him in a category essentially by himself. What happened to Diocles in the years following his retirement, whether he continued to reside in Rome, how he managed or invested the fortune his inscription records, and how long he lived beyond the erection of his own monument, remains largely unknown to us, swallowed by the same gaps in the historical record that obscure the private lives of even the most celebrated ancient individuals once they step outside the specific documentary spotlight, in his case a single extraordinary inscription, that happens to survive.

What Diocles leaves behind, in the end, is not really a biography in any full modern sense. It is a ledger, extraordinarily detailed for its time and remarkable even by modern standards of personal financial disclosure, that offers this book its single clearest and most concrete piece of evidence for exactly how much money genuinely moved through the Roman chariot racing industry, concentrated, in this one exceptionally well documented case, in the career earnings of one former provincial boy who rose, race by race, purse by purse, to a fortune that would have been the envy of senators. The following chapter turns from the earnings of the drivers themselves to the enormous and largely informal economy of private wagering that surrounded every race, an economy for which the evidence is considerably less tidy than Diocles' carefully inscribed monument, but which nonetheless left behind its own remarkable, if very different, category of physical evidence: curses, buried in lead and bronze, aimed at rival horses and drivers by fans and bettors desperate enough to seek supernatural intervention when ordinary skill and money were not enough to guarantee the outcome they wanted.

CHAPTER SIX

THE HOUSE ALWAYS WINS

A thin sheet of lead, folded twice and pierced through with an iron nail, buried in the packed earth near the starting gates of a North African circus sometime in the third century of the common era. Scratched into its surface, in Latin so clumsy and misspelled that it likely tells us more about the desperation of its author than his education, is a plea addressed not to any human authority but to the spirits of the underworld themselves: bind and weigh down the horses of the Blue and Red teams, the text demands, so that they cannot run, cannot obey the rein, cannot even move, but instead fall and shatter, dragging their drivers down with them, blinding them so they cannot see their rivals or find their way to victory.

This is a defixio, a curse tablet, and it belongs to a category of physical evidence that offers this book something the previous chapters, for all their reliance on inscriptions, agricultural treatises, and epigrammatic poetry, have not yet been able to provide: a direct, unmediated glimpse into the emotional intensity, and by clear implication the financial stakes, that ordinary Roman spectators attached to the outcome of individual chariot races. More than fifty such curse tablets have been recovered from the North African cities of

Hadrumetum and Carthage alone, discovered either buried in tombs or, more strikingly, planted directly at the racetrack itself, as close as the curse's author could physically get to the horses and drivers he was attempting to sabotage through supernatural means. Similar tablets have surfaced across the wider Roman world, though North Africa, for reasons scholars continue to debate, has yielded a disproportionately rich concentration of this particular category of evidence.

The tablets follow recognizable patterns, suggesting that a specialized trade of professional curse writers, magicians for hire who understood the correct formulas and vocesmagicae, the strange incantatory syllables believed to strengthen a curse's power, served clients seeking to gain an advantage, however illicit and however unlikely to actually influence the outcome, over their rivals at the track. One tablet recovered from Rome itself invokes holy angels and sacred names in a restraining spell aimed squarely at a charioteer named Eucherios and all of his horses, demanding that he be bound, struck down, and destroyed, that he fail to come from behind and pass his rivals but instead collapse and be broken, in both the early races of the day and the later ones. Another tablet from Hadrumetum curses the horses of the Green and White teams by name along with four specific charioteers, Clarus, Felix, Primulus, and Romanus, calling on unnamed spirits to torment and kill both animals and drivers alike from that very hour forward. These are not vague, generalized wishes for good fortune directed at a favored team. They are specific, targeted, often disturbingly violent attacks aimed at named individuals and named horses, commissioned by people who cared enough about the outcome of a specific race to pay for a professionally composed curse and risk discovery burying it in a location where it might actually be found and connected back to them.

What does this tell us about the economics of Roman chariot racing that the earlier chapters of this book, focused on factions, breeding operations, and driver earnings, have not already established? The answer lies in what these tablets imply about the scale and intensity of private betting surrounding every race, an activity ancient sources confirm was widespread across every level of Roman society but which, frustratingly for the economic historian, left behind almost none of the kind of formal financial documentation that would let us reconstruct betting volumes, typical wager sizes, or odds with anything approaching precision. Nobody buries a curse tablet, commissions a professional magician, and risks the social and legal consequences of practicing what Roman authorities generally regarded as illicit magic, over an outcome in which they have no genuine material stake. The specificity and sheer number of surviving circus curse tablets constitutes indirect but compelling evidence that private betting on chariot races involved sums significant enough, for at least some bettors, to justify this kind of extraordinary and risky countermeasure.

Roman sources are explicit that betting on chariot races was pervasive, cutting across social boundaries in a way that few other activities in Roman society managed to do. Emperors themselves were documented placing bets, senators wagered alongside common citizens in the stands, and the passionate, sometimes violent factional loyalty this book has already described in earlier chapters was inseparable from the financial stakes that spectators frequently attached to the outcome of individual races. What remains genuinely unclear, and here this book must exercise the same careful honesty about the limits of the evidence that has guided every previous chapter, is the precise mechanism through which this betting was actually conducted. Unlike a modern sportsbook operating through a licensed, centrally organized bookmaking apparatus, Roman betting on chariot races appears to have functioned as a largely decentralized, peer to peer activity, conducted directly between individual spectators or through informal intermediaries operating within the crowd, rather than through any formal betting apparatus controlled or operated by the racing factions themselves. There is no clear surviving evidence of anything resembling an official, faction sanctioned bookmaking operation comparable to what a modern reader might assume, given the scale of organized wagering activity that ancient sources otherwise describe.

This distinction matters enormously for understanding exactly how the financial benefits of widespread betting activity actually flowed through the chariot racing economy. If the factions themselves had operated formal bookmaking operations, this book could describe a direct, quantifiable revenue stream flowing from betting activity into faction coffers, comparable to the modern relationship between a sports league and licensed betting operators. The evidence available to us does not support that model. Instead, the benefit the factions derived from widespread private betting appears to have been considerably more indirect, though almost certainly no less real: betting intensified public engagement with individual races, transformed casual spectators into deeply invested partisans with genuine financial stakes riding on the outcome, drove attendance at major race days as bettors sought to watch events they had personal money riding on, and generally amplified exactly the kind of passionate factional loyalty that, as earlier chapters of this book have already established, translated into sustained public and imperial patronage for the factions that could most reliably command this level of devoted attention. Betting, in other words, functioned as a powerful multiplier of engagement and emotional investment even without any direct formal mechanism connecting individual wagers to faction revenue, and this indirect but substantial economic benefit should not be underestimated simply because it resists the kind of precise quantification that a formal, centrally organized betting industry would allow.

The curse tablets themselves offer a final, poignant category of evidence worth examining before this chapter moves on: the human desperation and genuine emotional investment that underlay all of this betting activity. These were not, for the most part, documents composed by wealthy senators with vast fortunes to spare on a single wager. The clumsy Latin, frequent misspellings, and formulaic reliance on hired professional curse writers found across the surviving corpus of circus defixiones suggest authorship spanning a considerably broader social range, including individuals for whom the outcome of a specific race, and whatever money they had riding on it, mattered enough to justify the expense and legal risk of commissioning a curse. Roman authorities did not look kindly on the practice of magic generally, and defixiones occupied legally ambiguous territory that could, in certain circumstances, expose their authors to real consequences if discovered and connected to accusations of malicious sorcery. That people continued to commission and bury these tablets in significant numbers across multiple centuries and multiple regions of the Roman world tells us something important about just how much emotional and financial weight ordinary Romans attached to the outcome of races that, from a distance of two thousand years, can look like nothing more than colorful ancient entertainment, but which functioned, for the people actually living through any given afternoon at the circus, as genuine occasions of real financial consequence and correspondingly intense emotional investment.

Curse tablets were not, it should be said clearly, the only method by which desperate bettors and faction partisans sought to influence a race's outcome, and the broader historical record preserves scattered but genuinely striking evidence of more direct, entirely secular forms of interference as well. Ancient sources describing the culture surrounding chariot racing reference practices that a modern reader will recognize immediately as recognizable forms of competitive corruption: horses allegedly drugged or otherwise tampered with before a race, rival charioteers approached with bribes to deliberately underperform or to obstruct a competitor during the chaotic scramble around the turning posts, and drivers occasionally accused, whether fairly or not, of accepting payment from opposing factions or wealthy bettors to influence a result in a direction that private wagers had already been placed to favor. A mosaic recovered from a faction training establishment in Roman Algeria, listing the extensive staff, jockeys, grooms, stable hands, saddlers, physicians, trainers, and messengers, employed in the maintenance of a single stable's operation, incidentally illustrates just how many individuals stood close enough to the horses and drivers at any given moment to make this kind of interference at least logistically plausible, even where the specific surviving accusations of doping or bribery resist the kind of forensic verification a modern reader might reasonably want before accepting them as established historical fact rather than colorful ancient rumor. What can be said with confidence is that the Romans themselves clearly believed such interference occurred with some regularity, a belief itself worth taking seriously as evidence, since a society does not generally develop persistent suspicions of race fixing and doping around an activity in which the financial stakes were genuinely trivial. The very existence of this suspicion, layered on top of the curse tablet evidence already examined in this chapter, reinforces the central argument this book has advanced from its opening pages: that Roman chariot racing involved sums of money substantial enough to make cheating, in whatever specific form it took, a rational calculation for at least some of the participants and interested parties surrounding any given race.

It would be a mistake, however, to treat the betting economy surrounding Roman chariot racing purely as a story of individual spectators wagering modest personal sums on the outcome of a single race, however revealing the curse tablets are about that particular layer of the phenomenon. Ancient satirical writers, particularly Juvenal in his biting descriptions of Roman social excess, suggest that wagering on the races could escalate into genuinely ruinous stakes for individuals who lost control of their gambling impulses, a pattern of behavior that, again, will strike a modern reader as uncomfortably familiar despite the two millennia separating ancient Rome from any contemporary sports betting market. The historical record does not allow us to quantify with any real precision what portion of ancient Roman households experienced genuine financial hardship as a direct result of chariot racing wagers gone wrong, but the persistent moral criticism directed at excessive gambling in Roman satirical and philosophical writing strongly suggests that this was a recognized and non trivial social problem, not merely a harmless diversion universally enjoyed without cost or consequence.

The picture that emerges from this chapter, then, is necessarily less precise and less quantifiable than the picture the previous chapter was able to construct around Diocles' meticulously inscribed career earnings. Where Diocles left behind a literal stone ledger, the Roman betting economy left behind curses, buried in lead, aimed at horses and drivers whose real crime, in the eyes of the tablets' authors, was simply competing against whichever team or driver that particular bettor had staked something valuable on. This is scattered, indirect, and inherently limited evidence, and any economic historian claiming to reconstruct precise betting volumes or typical wager sizes from this material alone would be overstating what the surviving record can actually bear. What the evidence does support, clearly and consistently across multiple regions and centuries of Roman history, is the conclusion that private wagering on chariot races was pervasive, socially significant, occasionally financially ruinous for individual participants, and, through the intensified public engagement and passionate factional loyalty it generated, an important if largely informal contributor to the overall commercial success of the racing industry described throughout this book. The house, in the sense of the four racing factions themselves, may not have operated a formal betting apparatus in anything like the modern sense. But the house, in a broader and ultimately more important sense, still won, because every wager placed, every curse tablet buried, and every fortune gained or lost on the outcome of a single race only deepened the public's devotion to an entertainment industry that had, by the height of the Roman Empire, become genuinely inseparable from Roman civic and financial life.

One final observation deserves a place in this chapter before it closes, because it speaks directly to the question of scale that has run throughout this book. The sheer geographic spread of the surviving curse tablet evidence, recovered not only from Rome and its immediate environs but from cities scattered across North Africa, Syria, and elsewhere in the Roman world, indicates that the private betting culture this chapter has described was never a phenomenon confined to the capital alone. Wherever the Romans built a circus and organized races under the four familiar colors, a parallel economy of private wagering, and evidently of private desperation intense enough to justify the expense and risk of a professionally composed curse, appears to have followed close behind. This geographic ubiquity matters because it confirms that the betting economy examined in this chapter was not a peculiarity of the capital's uniquely large and wealthy population, but a structural feature of chariot racing wherever the sport took root across the empire, replicated in provincial cities with a fraction of Rome's population and resources but, evidently, no less passionate an appetite for wagering on the outcome of a well matched race.

The next chapter turns from the private economy of individual wagers to the far larger and better documented economy of public funding, examining exactly how emperors, magistrates, and the Roman state itself underwrote an entertainment industry whose costs, by any measure, dwarfed the private betting economy this chapter has just described.

CHAPTER SEVEN

UNDERWRITING THE EMPIRE

Why would a Roman politician, ambitious for higher office but not yet independently wealthy enough to guarantee his own advancement, willingly bankrupt himself organizing a single afternoon of chariot races?

This question sits at the heart of one of the more counterintuitive aspects of Roman public finance, and answering it properly requires setting aside a modern assumption that most readers bring, often without realizing it, to the study of ancient spectacle: the assumption that games and entertainment represent a purely discretionary category of public spending, easily distinguished from the serious business of governing an empire. Roman elites did not see it that way, and neither, as this chapter will demonstrate, should we, if we want to understand how an enormous fraction of the ancient economy came to be organized around the funding of public entertainment on a scale that modern readers still find genuinely difficult to credit.

The formal machinery of public game funding in Rome centered, for much of the Republican period, on a magistracy called the aedileship. Aediles held responsibility for maintaining public buildings and spaces and for organizing the various public festivals, ludi, that punctuated the Roman calendar, and by the middle Republic these festivals occurred with real regularity, roughly ten to twelve times in an average year according to the surviving evidence, encompassing dramatic performances, chariot races, and eventually gladiatorial combat as well. Public funds were allocated to cover the basic costs of these mandated festivals, but ancient sources make clear that the officially budgeted amount routinely fell well short of what an ambitious aedile actually spent, since the political rewards of hosting a spectacularly memorable set of games could be substantial enough to justify considerable personal expenditure beyond the formal public allocation. This gap between public funding and actual expenditure is central to understanding the entire system: Roman public entertainment was never funded through a single, clean mechanism, but through an evolving and often deliberately ambiguous combination of state allocation and personal political investment, in which the individual sponsoring a set of games had every incentive to spend beyond what the treasury alone provided.

The financial burden of the aedileship became, by the final century of the Republic, so significant that ancient sources record individual politicians deliberately avoiding the office altogether specifically to escape the crushing expense of properly funding games at the level public expectation now demanded. This is a genuinely remarkable historical detail, worth pausing on for a moment: an entry level political office, one that in an earlier period had represented a reasonably modest financial obligation, had by the late Republic become so associated with lavish, expensive spectacle that some capable and ambitious men chose to bypass it entirely rather than risk financial ruin trying to meet the standard that previous aediles, competing with one another for public favor, had progressively driven ever higher. Polybius, the Greek historian who spent considerable time in Rome and wrote with genuine analytical insight about Roman institutions, records instances of individual Romans spending truly enormous sums on funeral games and associated spectacles during the middle Republic, and by the time we reach the political careers of figures like Julius Caesar in the first century before the common era, the scale of personal expenditure on public games had escalated to levels that ancient biographers describe, without obvious exaggeration, as genuinely ruinous for men who miscalculated their ability to recoup the political benefits of their spending.

This pattern of escalating, competitive expenditure on public games did not disappear with the transition from Republic to Empire. It simply shifted its primary source of funding from individual senatorial magistrates competing with one another for popular favor to the emperor himself, who now held a functional monopoly on the kind of truly spectacular, empire wide political capital that lavish public games could generate. The famous formulation attributed to the satirist Juvenal, writing in the late first or early second century, describing a Roman public that had traded genuine political engagement for the simple provision of bread and circuses, panem et circenses, captured with real precision a governing strategy that Roman emperors pursued deliberately and, by most measures, quite successfully across the following centuries. An emperor who reliably provided both subsidized grain, distributed through the annona system that supplied the city of Rome's enormous population, and spectacular, frequent public entertainment, purchased a form of political stability and popular goodwill that proved, time and again across Roman imperial history, considerably cheaper than the alternative of governing a chronically discontented and potentially rebellious urban population through coercion alone.

The specific costs involved, where ancient sources allow us to reconstruct them, illustrate just how significant an economic undertaking the funding of public games represented. Inscriptional evidence recording the summa honoraria, a formal payment that civic magistrates in cities across the Roman Empire were required to make upon entering office, often specifically earmarked toward the cost of public games, shows figures ranging widely depending on the wealth and status of the particular city and office in question, from a few thousand sesterces in smaller provincial towns to considerably larger sums in wealthier and more prestigious civic positions. One inscription from the North African city of Calama records a newly appointed pontifex, a religious official, paying six hundred thousand sesterces as an initiation payment, a figure that, while not exclusively earmarked for games funding, illustrates the general scale of wealth that Roman civic office increasingly required and that was frequently channeled, at least in part, toward the funding of public spectacle. Multiplied across the hundreds of cities scattered throughout the Roman Empire, each with its own civic magistrates expected to fund local games according to broadly similar principles, the aggregate sum flowing from private and public sources alike into the funding of public entertainment across the Roman world reached a scale that, however difficult to state with precise modern equivalence, clearly represented one of the single largest categories of discretionary economic activity in the entire ancient Mediterranean economy.

Individual emperors approached the question of games funding with noticeably different philosophies, and these differences offer a useful window into how seriously Roman rulers themselves understood the political economy of public spectacle. Augustus, the first emperor and a ruler acutely conscious of the delicate political theater required to stabilize a transition from republic to effectively monarchical rule, invested heavily and consistently in public games as part of a broader program of public works and civic patronage designed to cement his popular legitimacy. Tiberius, his successor, adopted a markedly more frugal approach that ancient biographers, not always sympathetically, record in considerable detail: reducing the pay allotted to performers, capping the number of gladiatorial pairs permitted at a given event, and generally attempting to rein in what he apparently regarded as an unsustainable trajectory of ever escalating public entertainment costs. That Tiberius's cost cutting measures became a notable and specifically recorded feature of his reign, remembered by later historians as a point of genuine contrast with his predecessor's more lavish approach, itself confirms just how central the scale of games spending had become to how Romans evaluated and remembered the character and priorities of their emperors. A ruler's approach to funding public spectacle was not a peripheral or trivial matter of personal taste. It was a defining feature of his broader political identity, scrutinized and remembered by contemporaries in terms not so different from how modern political commentary tracks a leader's approach to major public spending priorities.

The emperor Trajan, whose reign at the start of the second century this book's opening chapter already noted for the substantial expansion of the Circus Maximus itself, offers a particularly clear illustration of just how deliberately Roman emperors approached the political calculus of games funding. Ancient sources describing Trajan's reign consistently pair his investment in public spectacle with his equally substantial investment in the annona, the subsidized grain distribution system that fed Rome's enormous urban population, treating the two forms of expenditure as complementary halves of a single coherent strategy for maintaining popular loyalty. A population that was simultaneously well fed and well entertained, this strategy implicitly recognized, had correspondingly little practical incentive to translate whatever grievances it harbored into open political unrest, and emperors who funded both halves of this equation generously tended, as a matter of historical record, to enjoy considerably more stable reigns than those who neglected either one. This pairing of bread and circuses as twin pillars of imperial governance, rather than as two entirely separate categories of expenditure, helps explain why the funding of chariot racing specifically, as opposed to other forms of public entertainment, held such a privileged position in this broader strategy: chariot racing at the Circus Maximus reached a larger single audience in a single sitting than any other form of Roman public entertainment, making it, gladiatorial games and theatrical performances included, the single most efficient available instrument for demonstrating imperial generosity to the greatest possible number of Roman citizens simultaneously.

Later emperors, particularly through the height of the imperial period into the second and third centuries, generally trended back toward Augustus's more expansive model rather than Tiberius's austerity, and the scale of games, chariot races prominently among them, continued to grow across this period, driving parallel growth in the resources devoted to the four racing factions this book has already examined in detail. The relationship between imperial funding and faction prosperity was direct and mutually reinforcing: an emperor seeking to fund especially memorable and politically effective games needed factions capable of fielding genuinely spectacular racing competitions, complete with the finest horses, the most celebrated charioteers, and the kind of dramatic, closely contested races that would leave a lasting positive impression on the watching public. This gave the factions themselves, and particularly whichever faction currently held the strongest public following, real leverage in negotiating the terms of imperial patronage, since an emperor who allowed his games to become visibly inferior to those of a political rival, or simply to previous years' standards, risked exactly the kind of public disappointment that the entire system of spectacle funded political legitimacy was specifically designed to avoid.

It is worth stepping back at this point to consider the full scale of what this chapter has described, because the individual pieces, an ambitious aedile spending beyond his public allocation, a provincial pontifex paying a substantial initiation fee partly earmarked for local games, an emperor calculating the political return on a particularly lavish set of races, can obscure the genuinely staggering aggregate picture when considered only in isolation. Roman public entertainment, chariot racing very much included, represented one of the largest sustained categories of both public and quasi voluntary private expenditure in the entire ancient Mediterranean economy, rivaling in scale, if not necessarily exceeding, other major categories of Roman public investment like military expenditure or infrastructure construction. This was not incidental spending on frivolous amusement, tolerated by a serious governing class as an unfortunate but manageable indulgence of the masses. It was a deliberate, sustained, and enormously significant allocation of state and private resources, understood clearly by the Romans themselves as a direct and effective instrument of political governance, one that purchased public stability and popular loyalty with a reliability that more conventional forms of political engagement, elections, senatorial debate, direct appeals to civic virtue, had proven considerably less capable of guaranteeing on their own.

It is worth adding, finally, that this entire system of games funding operated within a broader Roman fiscal environment that lacked almost every institutional tool a modern government would use to manage large scale public expenditure. There was no equivalent of a modern national budget process weighing games funding against competing priorities in any systematic, centrally coordinated fashion, no bond market through which a magistrate or emperor could smooth the timing of a large one time expenditure across multiple years, and no professional civil service bureaucracy dedicated specifically to overseeing entertainment spending with the kind of specialized administrative expertise a modern sports ministry or municipal stadium authority might bring to the task. Instead, the entire apparatus this chapter has described operated through a combination of individual political ambition, competitive social pressure among elites eager to be remembered for their generosity, and, at the imperial level, a ruler's personal judgment about how much of the state's resources a given set of games justified relative to other pressing priorities like military campaigns or infrastructure projects. That this comparatively improvised system nonetheless managed to sustain, across many centuries, a level of public entertainment spending that this chapter has argued rivaled other major categories of ancient state expenditure, is itself a genuinely remarkable testament to how deeply the underlying political logic of spectacle funded legitimacy had embedded itself in Roman governing culture, operating effectively even without the kind of formal institutional machinery that a modern observer might assume such a large and sustained category of public spending would require.

This is, ultimately, the deepest sense in which the title of this book should be understood. Chariot racing was not merely an industry that happened to generate substantial private wealth for faction owners and successful charioteers, remarkable as those individual fortunes genuinely were. It was an industry that the Roman state itself, from individual aediles competing for popular favor in the late Republic through to emperors managing the political stability of an empire spanning three continents, understood as a direct and indispensable instrument of governance, worthy of an allocation of public and private resources that few other categories of ancient economic activity could match. The financial empire this book has been describing did not exist at arm's length from Roman political power. It was, in the most literal and consequential sense, underwritten by that power, and it repaid the investment, across centuries of sustained public spectacle, with a currency far more valuable to any ruling class than money alone: the simple, durable political loyalty of a Roman public that had every reason, watching the horses thunder around the spina of the Circus Maximus, to feel that its government was providing, however imperfectly, for its most cherished collective pleasures.

The following chapter turns to what happened when this carefully cultivated loyalty curdled into something far more dangerous, examining the racing factions not merely as commercial and entertainment enterprises but as genuine political and social power blocs capable of organizing urban violence on a scale that could, in the most extreme documented case, threaten the very stability of an emperor's rule.

CHAPTER EIGHT

THE RIOT ECONOMY

Nika.

Win.

For centuries, this single Greek word had echoed through the Hippodrome of Constantinople as nothing more sinister than the standard cheer of an excited racing crowd, shouted by tens of thousands of throats urging their favored charioteer toward the finish line. On the thirteenth of January in the year 532, the crowd inside that same Hippodrome shouted it again, but this time the word was not aimed at any driver on the track. It had become, in the space of a single afternoon, a battle cry, and by the time the violence it announced had finally burned itself out five days later, an estimated thirty thousand people lay dead, vast sections of Constantinople had been reduced to ash, and the reign of one of the most consequential rulers in Byzantine history had come within a hair's breadth of collapsing entirely.

This chapter examines the racing factions not as the commercial and entertainment enterprises this book has focused on so far, but as genuine political and social power blocs, capable of mobilizing collective action on a scale that could threaten, and very nearly did overthrow, the government of the eastern Roman Empire itself. Understanding how a sporting rivalry could escalate into an event of this magnitude requires first understanding just how deeply the factional loyalties this book has already described in earlier chapters had fused, by the sixth century, with genuine social and political identity in a way that transcended anything modern readers typically associate with sports fandom.

By the time of the events this chapter examines, the four factions of earlier Roman history had consolidated, in the eastern Mediterranean, into two dominant blocs. The Greens had absorbed the Reds, and the Blues had absorbed the Whites, leaving a rivalry structure considerably simpler and, if anything, more intensely polarized than the four way competition that had characterized the sport during the height of the western Roman Empire. This consolidation, consistent with the general pattern of market concentration this book noted in an earlier chapter examining the original four factions, had concentrated an enormous share of public loyalty and passionate identification into just two competing organizations, and by the reign of the emperor Justinian, who came to power in the year 527, these two factions had become associated with broader currents of social and political division within Constantinopolitan society that extended well beyond simple preferences about which team's horses ran faster. Ancient sources, particularly the historian Procopius, whose sometimes unreliable but genuinely well informed contemporary account remains our single richest source for the events of 532, describe the Blues as generally associated with more established, conservative elements of Constantinopolitan society, including, notably, Justinian himself, a well known partisan supporter of the Blue faction even after ascending to the imperial throne, while the Greens drew disproportionate support from a broader popular base, giving the two factions a social and political texture that went well beyond mere athletic rivalry.

The immediate spark for the crisis of 532 involved neither high politics nor deep social grievance in any abstract sense, but rather a very concrete and specific miscarriage of justice connected directly to ordinary factional violence. In the days before the riot, several members of both the Blue and Green factions had been arrested following disturbances connected to the ordinary, chronic pattern of violence between rival faction supporters that Roman and Byzantine authorities had struggled to control for generations. The city prefect responsible for law and order in Constantinople, a man named Eudaemon, ordered a group of these arrested rioters executed on the tenth of January. The execution, carried out by hanging, went badly wrong: the scaffold or gallows apparatus failed, and two of the condemned men, one a Blue supporter and one a Green, survived the botched execution and were rescued by sympathetic monks, who spirited them away to the sanctuary of a nearby church, which imperial soldiers then surrounded and placed under guard.

What happened next reveals, with unusual clarity, exactly how the entrenched factional structures this book has traced across earlier chapters could function as a preexisting infrastructure for organized political action, mobilized almost instantly once a genuine grievance presented itself. Three days later, on the thirteenth of January, both the Blue and Green factions, still bitter rivals in every ordinary sense and typically far more likely to riot against one another than in common cause, appeared together at the Hippodrome during the day's scheduled races and began appealing directly to Justinian, seated in the imperial box overlooking the track, to pardon the two men who had survived their execution. According to Byzantine chronicler John Malalas, whose account of the crisis survives in useful if not always perfectly reliable detail, the crowd continued its appeals through race after race, twenty two of the twenty four scheduled events passing without any response from the emperor. When Justinian finally did respond, it was not with the mercy the crowd sought.

The refusal transformed the character of the crowd's demands almost instantly. Rather than continuing to appeal separately as Blues and Greens, the two factions, according to the ancient sources describing these events, spontaneously united, their traditional and often violent rivalry set aside in the face of shared grievance against imperial authority, and began chanting the word that gives this catastrophic episode its name: Nika. Win. What had begun as a specific appeal for clemency toward two individual prisoners rapidly escalated into a broader expression of accumulated political grievance, one that historians studying the period connect to genuine and longstanding popular discontent over heavy taxation, particularly taxation associated with the praetorian prefect John the Cappadocian, whose aggressive fiscal policies, implemented to help fund Justinian's ambitious and expensive military campaigns aimed at reconquering territory in the western Mediterranean, had generated substantial resentment among Constantinople's population well before the specific spark of the botched executions ignited open revolt.

The violence that followed consumed Constantinople for the better part of a week. The united factions burned the headquarters of the city prefect who had ordered the original executions. When Justinian attempted to defuse the growing crisis by proceeding with games on the following day as though nothing unusual had occurred, a decision that in retrospect reads as a serious political misjudgment of the crowd's mood, the response was further arson rather than pacification, with fires spreading through significant portions of the city, ultimately consuming, among many other structures, the great church of Hagia Sophia, whose destruction in these riots necessitated the construction of the even more magnificent structure that stands, rebuilt under Justinian's own subsequent orders, in Istanbul to this day. For several days, the rioters effectively controlled significant portions of Constantinople, and at the crisis's most dangerous point, they proclaimed an alternative claimant to the imperial throne, a nephew of a previous emperor named Hypatius, who found himself, according to some ancient accounts more a reluctant hostage of circumstance than an eager usurper, elevated by the mob to a position that placed his own life in mortal danger regardless of how the crisis ultimately resolved.

Justinian, according to the tradition preserved in several ancient sources, seriously considered fleeing the city as the situation deteriorated, a decision that would very likely have ended his reign permanently even if he had survived the immediate crisis. It was, according to this same tradition, his wife, the empress Theodora, who persuaded him to remain and confront the rebellion directly, reportedly declaring, in a speech ancient historians recorded though modern scholars debate its precise verbatim accuracy, that the imperial purple made a fine burial shroud and that she herself would never live to see the day when she was not addressed as empress, a formulation that, whatever its exact historical authenticity, captures accurately enough the resolve that ultimately kept Justinian in Constantinople rather than fleeing into ignominious exile.

The resolution, when it came, was swift and brutally decisive. Justinian's generals, most notably Belisarius, one of the most capable military commanders of the entire Byzantine period, led loyal troops into the Hippodrome, where a substantial portion of the rebellious crowd had gathered, and proceeded to slaughter the assembled crowd in a massacre that ancient sources place at approximately thirty thousand deaths, a figure that, whatever precise accuracy we grant it given the inherent difficulty of ancient casualty estimates, represents one of the most severe single episodes of urban violence recorded anywhere in ancient or late antique history. Hypatius, the reluctant imperial claimant elevated by the mob, was captured and executed on Justinian's orders shortly afterward, eliminating any lingering threat of a rival claim to the throne.

Modern historians studying the institutional structure underlying the Nika crisis have emphasized that the racing factions of sixth century Constantinople functioned, by this point in their long institutional development, as something considerably more formalized than the purely commercial entities this book's second chapter described in the context of the earlier Roman Republic and early Empire. The factions had become closely intertwined with the demes, urban militia and civic organizational structures that carried genuine responsibilities for aspects of city defense and public order alongside their continued role as the organizing bodies for chariot racing competition. This institutional evolution meant that the Blues and Greens of sixth century Constantinople possessed something the four factions of earlier Roman history had never quite developed to the same degree: a standing, organized capacity for collective action that extended well beyond the racetrack itself, encompassing structures of local leadership, communication, and coordinated response that could be, and evidently was, redirected toward open political rebellion once sufficient grievance had accumulated to trigger it. This helps explain why the Nika crisis escalated with such extraordinary speed once the initial spark of the botched executions had been struck. The two factions were not, in January of 532, spontaneously improvising a novel form of collective action from nothing. They were activating and redirecting an existing organizational infrastructure, built up over generations of managing the logistics of chariot racing itself, toward a purpose considerably more dangerous than anything its original commercial and sporting functions had ever required.

What does an episode of this magnitude and horror tell us about the economics of chariot racing that this book has been examining across its preceding chapters? The answer operates on several levels simultaneously, and each deserves careful attention rather than a single simplified conclusion. First, and most directly, the Nika riots demonstrate with stark clarity exactly how much genuine social and political capital had accumulated within the structure of the racing factions by the sixth century, capital built, this book has argued throughout, on a foundation of sustained commercial investment in breeding operations, driver development, and public spectacle stretching back many centuries. The factions were not simply entertainment providers whose influence began and ended at the edge of the racetrack. They had become, through the accumulated weight of that sustained economic and cultural investment, genuine organizing structures for urban political identity, capable of mobilizing coordinated collective action at a scale and speed that more conventional Byzantine political institutions could rarely match.

Second, the aftermath of the riots reveals just how seriously the imperial government itself took this concentration of factional power once its full danger had been demonstrated beyond any possibility of denial. Justinian, having survived what came perilously close to being the end of his reign, moved in the following years to curtail the independent political and social influence of the racing factions more systematically, even as he continued, in a pattern consistent with the broader argument this book has made about the political value of public spectacle, to fund and support chariot racing itself as an ongoing feature of Byzantine public life. This was not, in other words, a case of an emperor concluding that the underlying commercial and entertainment enterprise of chariot racing was itself the problem to be eliminated. It was a far more targeted recognition that the accumulated social and political power the factions had built up around that commercial enterprise, power this book has traced developing gradually across many centuries of sustained investment and public loyalty, required more careful management and containment going forward, lest a future crisis produce an outcome less favorable to the reigning emperor than Justinian, through a combination of

Theodora's resolve and Belisarius's military competence, had managed to secure.

Third, and finally, the economic cost of the riots themselves deserves acknowledgment, even though ancient sources do not provide anything resembling a precise formal accounting of the total financial damage inflicted on Constantinople during this catastrophic week. The destruction of major public buildings, including the original Hagia Sophia, the loss of an estimated thirty thousand lives representing an enormous toll in terms of lost productive labor and human capital, and the general disruption of commercial activity throughout the city during the period of active violence, all represent genuine and substantial economic costs, imposed directly by a crisis that originated in, and was executed through, the organizational infrastructure of the racing factions this book has spent its preceding chapters describing in far more benign commercial terms. The same structures of loyalty, organization, and mobilized collective identity that generated enormous commercial value for the factions and enormous political value for the emperors who funded them could, when circumstances aligned badly enough, generate catastrophic destruction instead, and this dual capacity, for tremendous constructive economic and political value on the one hand and for catastrophic destructive violence on the other, is perhaps the single most important lesson the Nika riots offer for anyone seeking to understand the true scale and significance of the financial and social empire built around Roman and Byzantine chariot racing.

The Hippodrome of Constantinople, like the Circus Maximus that preceded it and inspired its design, was never merely a racetrack. It was, this chapter has argued, one of the primary organizing institutions of an entire late antique urban society, and the events of January 532 stand as the starkest possible demonstration of exactly how much power, for good and for catastrophic ill alike, had come to be concentrated within its walls. The following chapter steps back from this extreme case of factional violence to examine the broader, generally less catastrophic but no less economically significant phenomenon of fan culture and factional identity, tracing how ordinary Roman spectators expressed and sustained their loyalty to a favored color across the long stretches of ordinary life that fell between such dramatic and violent crises.

CHAPTER NINE

MERCHANDISE OF THE MOB

Somewhere in the ruins of ancient Aphrodisias, a city in what is now western Turkey, archaeologists working through the site's public spaces uncovered a scattering of graffiti scratched into stone by residents who lived there some seventeen centuries ago. The messages are brief, often little more than a sentence, but their content will strike any modern sports fan as immediately, almost startlingly familiar. Victory for the Red, reads one. Bad years for the Greens, complains another. The fortune of the Blues prevails, boasts a third. These are not formal inscriptions commissioned by wealthy patrons or civic authorities. They are the ancient equivalent of a fan scrawling a team's name on a wall or carving initials into a stadium seat, spontaneous, unofficial, and unmistakably genuine expressions of exactly the kind of passionate personal investment in a sports team's fortunes that anyone who has ever followed professional athletics will recognize immediately across the gulf of two thousand years.

This chapter turns from the large scale commercial and political structures examined in previous chapters, the factions themselves, their breeding operations, their relationship to imperial funding, toward something smaller in scale but no less economically significant in its own way: the vast, informal economy of fan culture and popular identification that surrounded Roman chariot racing at every level of society, from the graffiti scratched by ordinary residents of provincial cities to the elaborate decorative mosaics commissioned by wealthy villa owners to celebrate their favorite drivers and horses. This popular culture surrounding the sport was not a peripheral curiosity. It was, this chapter will argue, an essential part of the mechanism by which the racing factions sustained the kind of deep, generational public loyalty that translated, as earlier chapters have already established, into continued public and imperial investment across the many centuries of the sport's dominance.

Consider first the sheer physical ubiquity of chariot racing imagery across the material culture of the Roman world. Charioteers and their horses appeared on oil lamps used for ordinary household lighting, on decorative glass bowls, on the carved handles of everyday knives, and, in their most elaborate and expensive form, on the floor mosaics that wealthy Roman and provincial elites commissioned to decorate their private villas. Archaeologists working across North Africa, a region that has yielded a particularly rich concentration of circus themed decorative art, have recovered numerous mosaics depicting named charioteers and named horses in vivid, carefully rendered detail. A mosaic from a villa at Baccano in Italy, dating to the third century of the common era, depicts a charioteer and horse from each of the four traditional factions arranged together, a kind of formal portrait gallery celebrating the sport's complete competitive landscape rather than favoring any single team. Other mosaics, from sites at Thuburbo Majus in modern Tunisia and from villas across Roman Spain, capture specific dramatic moments: a victorious Green charioteer receiving his prize, chariots locked in mid race competition around the spina. These were not cheap decorative choices. Mosaic work of this quality and scale represented a substantial investment by the villa owners who commissioned it, and the fact that so many wealthy Romans across such a geographically dispersed range of the empire chose to spend considerable sums memorializing chariot racing specifically, rather than any of the numerous other subjects available to Roman decorative art, testifies powerfully to just how central the sport had become to elite as well as popular Roman cultural identity.

The economic implications of this ubiquitous imagery deserve more careful attention than they typically receive in popular accounts of Roman entertainment culture. Every oil lamp molded with a charioteer's image, every mosaic commissioned to celebrate a favorite faction, every carved knife handle depicting a famous horse, represented genuine economic activity: skilled craftsmen employed, raw materials purchased, finished goods sold to consumers willing to pay for the privilege of surrounding themselves, in their most intimate domestic spaces, with reminders of their sporting loyalties. This constitutes, in effect, an ancient merchandising economy, considerably less organized and centrally controlled than the licensed merchandising operations that generate substantial revenue for modern professional sports franchises, but functioning through essentially the same underlying commercial logic: intense fan loyalty creates sustained consumer demand for objects that allow fans to express and reinforce that loyalty in their everyday lives, and craftsmen and merchants across the Roman world responded to that demand by producing an enormous volume of chariot racing themed goods across every price point, from the simplest mass produced terracotta lamp affordable to an ordinary urban resident to the most elaborate commissioned villa mosaic available only to the wealthiest elite.

Children's culture offers a particularly striking window into just how thoroughly factional identity had permeated Roman society by the height of the imperial period. Archaeological evidence indicates that children played with toy chariots, some inscribed with the names of celebrated real world charioteers, suggesting that fan identification with the sport's biggest stars began remarkably early in a typical Roman childhood and was actively cultivated, whether by parents purchasing these toys or by the broader commercial culture producing them, well before a child would have been old enough to attend and fully appreciate an actual race at the Circus Maximus. This pattern of childhood identification with sporting heroes, familiar to any parent in the modern world who has purchased a jersey or action figure bearing the name of a favorite athlete for a young child, turns out to have a documented precedent stretching back nearly two millennia, and it illustrates how deeply and how early Roman commercial culture worked to cultivate exactly the kind of lifelong factional loyalty that, as previous chapters have established, translated directly into sustained public investment in the sport across successive generations.

The scale of this material culture industry deserves one further observation before this chapter turns to the more spontaneous evidence of graffiti. Every one of the countless lamps, mosaics, glass bowls, and knife handles decorated with faction colors and celebrated charioteers required, as a basic precondition of manufacture, a reliable supply of the specific pigments and materials needed to render red, white, blue, and green in a form that Roman consumers would recognize immediately as denoting a specific faction. This was not a trivial manufacturing consideration in the ancient world, where certain dyes and pigments, blue derived from imported indigo or from the mineral azurite, in particular, could carry a meaningfully higher production cost than more readily available reds and whites drawn from more common mineral and organic sources. Some modern historians studying the material evidence have speculated, though the surviving documentation does not allow this to be stated with complete certainty, that the relative cost and availability of faction associated pigments and dyes may have subtly influenced which colors appeared more frequently in certain categories of mass produced decorative goods across different regions of the empire, with cheaper, more universally available reds and whites potentially appearing somewhat more often in the least expensive tier of merchandise available to ordinary urban consumers. Whatever the precise truth of this specific pricing dynamic, the broader point stands clearly enough on its own: an entire secondary manufacturing economy, encompassing potters, glassmakers, mosaic artisans, and metalworkers, had grown up specifically to supply the popular demand for chariot racing themed material culture this chapter has been describing, and this secondary economy, like the breeding operations examined in this book's third chapter, represents another layer of genuine commercial activity generated by the sport that extended well beyond the formal structure of the four factions themselves.

Graffiti, as the opening example from Aphrodisias demonstrates, offers perhaps our richest and most immediate surviving evidence of genuine, spontaneous popular sentiment surrounding the sport, precisely because it required no significant financial investment and no commercial motive, representing instead the direct, unmediated voice of ordinary Roman spectators expressing their feelings in the most casual and unguarded medium available to them. Pompeii, the city famously preserved by the eruption of Mount Vesuvius in the year 79, has yielded particularly vivid examples of this genre. One surviving piece of graffiti celebrates a charioteer named Crescens, a driver associated with the Blue faction, in terms that a modern reader will recognize instantly as the ancient equivalent of celebrity fandom, declaring that this charioteer held the affections of all the city's young women, a boast that speaks as much to the genuine celebrity status successful charioteers achieved among the Roman public, a theme this book examined in detail in its chapters on individual driver careers, as it does to the specific romantic claims being made. Similar graffiti recovered from Aphrodisias, cited at the opening of this chapter, and from numerous other sites across the Roman world, consistently displays this same pattern: brief, emotionally direct expressions of factional loyalty or disappointment, scratched into public walls by residents who felt strongly enough about their team's fortunes to record that feeling permanently, in whatever medium was immediately available to them.

The intensity of this popular identification carried real social consequences that extended well beyond the collection of decorative objects and the scratching of graffiti, consequences that connect directly back to the pattern of factional violence this book examined in detail in its previous chapter's account of the Nika riots. Faction loyalty, as multiple ancient sources attest, functioned as a genuine social dividing line within Roman urban communities, comparable in its intensity to religious or, in some documented instances, ethnic identity in other historical contexts. A person who supported the Green faction, ancient sources suggest, did not easily or comfortably socialize with a committed supporter of the Blues, and violence between rival faction supporters, in the stands during races and in the streets afterward, represented a persistent and genuinely serious drain on the law enforcement resources available to Roman civic authorities across the empire, well before the specific catastrophic escalation examined in the previous chapter's account of Constantinople in 532. Supporters are recorded burning symbols associated with rival factions and ambushing opposing fans in the aftermath of particularly contentious race results, a pattern of low level but persistent social conflict that, however troubling from a modern perspective concerned with public order, also testifies powerfully to just how genuinely and how widely the passionate factional identification this chapter has been describing had spread across Roman society, at every social level from the enslaved spectators packed into the Circus Maximus's upper tiers to senators and, on well documented occasions, emperors themselves.

This deep well of popular sentiment, cultivated across generations through the everyday material culture this chapter has surveyed, from children's toys to household lamps to villa mosaics to spontaneous graffiti, constituted, this book argues, an economic asset of genuine and substantial value to the racing factions, even though it resists the kind of precise financial quantification that this book has been able to apply to other aspects of the chariot racing economy, such as Diocles' meticulously inscribed prize winnings examined in an earlier chapter. Sustained, intergenerational public loyalty of this depth and intensity is precisely the kind of asset that guaranteed continued attendance at races, continued public and imperial willingness to fund increasingly lavish spectacle, and continued commercial demand for the enormous range of chariot racing themed goods that craftsmen and merchants across the Roman world produced to meet an apparently inexhaustible public appetite. Modern sports marketing executives spend enormous sums and considerable strategic effort attempting to cultivate exactly this kind of deep emotional brand loyalty among fans, and it is worth appreciating that the Roman racing factions appear to have achieved a comparable, and in some respects an even more intense, level of genuine popular devotion with a set of promotional tools, decorative art, casual graffiti, children's toys, and above all the simple, repeated spectacle of competitive racing itself, that would strike a modern marketing professional as almost primitively simple by comparison with the sophisticated tools available to a contemporary sports franchise.

What this chapter has tried to demonstrate, in sum, is that the financial empire this book has been tracing across its preceding chapters did not rest solely on the formal, quantifiable transactions this book has examined in greatest detail: prize purses, imperial subsidies, breeding contracts, and the like. It rested equally, and in some respects more fundamentally, on an enormous, diffuse, and largely informal economy of popular sentiment and material culture, one that reproduced and reinforced factional loyalty across every level of Roman society and across successive generations, ensuring that the commercial and political structures examined elsewhere in this book had a genuinely inexhaustible reservoir of public devotion to draw upon. The graffiti scratched into a wall in Aphrodisias, declaring bad years for the Greens or the enduring fortune of the Blues, represents, in its own small and unofficial way, as genuine a piece of evidence for the scale and depth of the Roman chariot racing economy as Diocles' carefully inscribed monument or the summa honoraria payments recorded in provincial civic inscriptions. It is simply evidence of a different kind, capturing not the movement of money through formal channels but the accumulated weight of ordinary human passion that made all of that formal financial activity possible and, ultimately, worthwhile.

It is also worth noting that this popular material culture was never confined to Rome and Italy alone, a point that reinforces an argument this book has made repeatedly across its preceding chapters about the genuinely empire wide scale of the chariot racing phenomenon. The mosaics recovered from North Africa, the graffiti preserved at Aphrodisias in Asia Minor, and comparable finds from Roman Britain, Gaul, and Spain together demonstrate that a resident of almost any substantial city within the empire's borders could participate in essentially the same culture of factional identification, decorative commemoration, and casual public expression of sporting loyalty that this chapter has documented in such detail. A traveler moving from a provincial city in North Africa to Rome itself, or from Britain to Antioch, would have found the same four colors, the same basic vocabulary of victory and defeat, and very possibly some of the same celebrated charioteer names recognized and celebrated across an extraordinary geographic range. Few other cultural phenomena in the ancient world achieved this degree of genuinely uniform recognition across such vast distances, and it stands as one of the more striking testaments to just how effectively the commercial and cultural machinery this book has examined succeeded in exporting a coherent, recognizable product across the entire breadth of Roman territory.

The following chapter turns to a considerably darker aspect of this same passionate, high stakes world: the genuine physical risks faced by everyone involved in the industry, from charioteers to horses, and the ways in which Roman society calculated, priced, and managed the constant presence of injury and death that shadowed even the most celebrated careers this book has described.

CHAPTER TEN

THE ACTUARIES OF THE SAND

Flavius Scorpus died at twenty seven years old, having spent his brief adult life accumulating two thousand and forty eight victories for the Green faction, a career record so extraordinary in its sheer volume of winning that ancient poets, Martial prominent among them, wrote of him with a mixture of genuine admiration and something closer to unease at how much fortune and fame had been compressed into a life cut short so young. Born, like so many successful charioteers this book has already discussed, in the Roman province of Hispania, and enslaved for at least part of his working life, Scorpus achieved earnings that ancient sources suggest exceeded those of professional Roman sponsors, individuals of genuine wealth and social standing in their own right, a comparison that underscores once again just how dramatically the economics of celebrity spectacle diverged from ordinary patterns of wealth accumulation in the ancient world. And then, having achieved all of this by an age when many Roman men of more conventional careers were only beginning to establish themselves professionally, he was gone.

Scorpus's death is not an isolated anomaly in the historical record of Roman chariot racing. It is, this chapter argues, close to the statistical norm for a profession whose economic rewards, as previous chapters have documented in considerable detail, cannot be properly understood in isolation from the mortal risk that made those rewards possible in the first place. This chapter turns directly to that risk, examining what the surviving evidence can tell us about the actual life expectancy and injury patterns of professional charioteers, and considering how Roman society itself understood, priced, and managed the constant presence of death that shadowed even the most celebrated careers this book has described.

Reconstructing precise mortality statistics for any occupational group in the ancient world presents genuine methodological challenges that responsible historians must acknowledge rather than paper over with false statistical confidence. Roman tombstones and epitaphs, our primary surviving source for ages at death across the ancient population generally, suffer from well documented biases: they systematically underrepresent infant and child mortality, they show a persistent pattern of age exaggeration among the elderly, seemingly reflecting a very human impulse to inflate one's longevity for posterity, and they overwhelmingly represent individuals whose families or communities could afford the expense of a commemorative inscription in the first place, meaning the poorest members of

Roman society, a category that would have included many charioteers at the outset of their careers, are almost certainly underrepresented in the surviving epigraphic record. Modern demographic historians studying these patterns generally estimate life expectancy at birth for the urban population of the western Roman Empire during the first and second centuries somewhere between fifteen and twenty five years, a figure heavily depressed by catastrophic infant and child mortality rather than reflecting the actual life course a person could reasonably expect if they survived past early childhood, with overall empire wide life expectancy estimated somewhat higher, in the range of twenty five to thirty years, once the full population is considered.

Against this general demographic backdrop, what can we say specifically about charioteers? The occupation involved risks that went well beyond the ordinary hazards of disease, malnutrition, and violence that shaped Roman mortality patterns generally, and the specific mechanics of those risks, described in an earlier chapter's account of the reins wrapped around a driver's waist and the falx knife carried specifically to cut free from a fatal tangle, were substantial enough that ancient sources treat the early death of a celebrated charioteer not as a shocking aberration but as an almost expected, if still genuinely mourned, occupational hazard.

Scorpus's death at twenty seven stands alongside other documented cases of charioteers dying young, in the prime of celebrated careers, at ages that would represent a genuinely tragic loss in any historical context but that occur with sufficient frequency in the surviving record of Roman chariot racing to constitute a recognizable pattern rather than a series of isolated misfortunes.

It is worth pausing to consider precisely what made chariot racing so much more physically dangerous than most other Roman occupations, since the specific mechanics of the risk illuminate exactly why the financial rewards this book has documented in such detail needed to be as substantial as they were in order to sustain a continuous supply of willing, or at least compelled, participants. The turns around the metae at either end of the central spina represented the single most dangerous moment of any race, the point at which multiple chariots, often four or more competing teams, converged at high speed into a tight turning radius, each driver attempting to take the innermost and therefore shortest possible line while his rivals pressed just as aggressively for the same advantage. Collisions at this point in the race, referred to in Latin sources by a term, naufragia, that literally means shipwrecks, a metaphor vivid enough to convey the sheer chaotic violence of a chariot race gone wrong, could involve multiple teams tangled together, horses panicking and thrashing amid wreckage, and drivers dragged across the packed sand by animals that no longer responded to any attempt at control. A driver caught in a naufragium faced genuine mortal danger regardless of his skill or experience, since the outcome depended as much on the specific physics of a given collision, how his chariot's wheels caught the ground, whether his falx knife came free of his belt quickly enough to cut the tangled reins, as on any factor within his own control.

The economic logic underlying this brutal calculus deserves direct examination, uncomfortable as the subject necessarily is. Faction owners, this book has established in earlier chapters, invested substantially in identifying, training, and developing promising young charioteers, an investment that represented genuine sunk capital exposed to the very real risk of sudden and total loss whenever a driver suffered a fatal or career ending injury. This risk almost certainly factored into how factions approached their broader talent development strategy, likely encouraging the kind of continuous pipeline of new young drivers described in an earlier chapter's discussion of the labor market for charioteers, since no individual driver, however talented, could be relied upon as a permanent, risk free asset. The prize money and eventual path to freedom available to successful drivers, examined in detail in this book's fourth chapter, functioned in part as compensation for exactly this mortal risk, a form of hazard pay that, in the case of the most successful drivers like Diocles, who survived his entire twenty four year career to retire at forty two, could reach truly extraordinary heights precisely because so many of his contemporaries and rivals never lived to enjoy anything comparable.

This raises an uncomfortable but historically important question that this book has touched on in earlier chapters and must now address directly: did the enormous financial rewards available to successful charioteers represent a form of consent, however constrained by the underlying reality of enslaved status, to accept genuinely mortal occupational risk in exchange for otherwise unattainable wealth and social mobility? The honest answer, consistent with this book's broader commitment to acknowledging genuine complexity rather than imposing a falsely simple moral narrative onto historical evidence that does not support one, is that the relationship between charioteers and the factions that owned or employed them cannot be reduced to a straightforward story of either pure exploitation or pure opportunity. Most charioteers began their careers enslaved, with no meaningful choice in the matter of entering an occupation that would very likely kill them before they reached their thirties. At the same time, the specific structure of financial reward and the documented pathway toward eventual manumission, examined in this book's fourth chapter, created genuine incentives that, once a driver had begun his career, shaped his subsequent choices, including, quite plausibly, decisions about which tactical risks to take in pursuit of the largest prize purses, in ways that combined coercion and opportunity in a manner that resists easy moral categorization from a distance of nearly two thousand years.

The medical response available to an injured charioteer, while primitive by any modern clinical standard, was not entirely absent, and its existence tells us something further about how seriously the factions treated their human capital investment. This book's second chapter already noted the presence of medici, medical specialists, among the documented staff of a major Roman racing faction, individuals whose responsibilities evidently extended to treating injured drivers as well as injured horses. Roman medicine of this period, while lacking anything resembling modern trauma surgery, anesthesia, or infection control, did possess a genuine and, by ancient standards, reasonably sophisticated body of practical knowledge concerning the setting of broken bones, the treatment of wounds, and general convalescent care, knowledge that a faction's medical staff would have applied regularly given the routine frequency of injury this chapter has already documented. That factions maintained dedicated medical staff at all, rather than simply discarding injured drivers to fend for themselves, reflects the same underlying economic logic this chapter has traced throughout: a faction had made a substantial training investment in any driver who had progressed far enough to compete regularly, and a broken bone or a serious but survivable wound represented a temporary interruption to that investment's return rather than, as an outright fatality would, its complete and total loss. The presence of these medical staff should not be romanticized into anything resembling genuine ancient sports medicine in the modern therapeutic sense, but neither should it be dismissed as entirely absent from the calculus of how factions managed the very real physical toll this chapter has documented.

The horses themselves, it is worth adding, faced comparable risks, and the previous chapters' extensive discussion of the breeding economy that supplied circus horses takes on additional weight when considered alongside the physical dangers those animals faced once their training was complete and their racing careers began. A horse injured or killed in a naufragium represented a direct financial loss to the faction that owned it, comparable in scale, given the substantial investment in breeding, transport, and training described in this book's third chapter, to the loss of a valuable piece of capital equipment in any other Roman commercial enterprise. This economic reality likely shaped training and racing decisions in ways the surviving evidence allows us only to infer rather than document with precision: a faction balancing the potential rewards of racing a particularly valuable horse in a high stakes event against the risk of losing that same animal to injury was engaged in exactly the kind of risk management calculation that any capital intensive commercial enterprise, ancient or modern, must continuously perform.

What emerges from this examination is a picture of an industry whose extraordinary financial rewards, documented throughout this book in figures that still strain modern credulity, existed in direct and inseparable relationship to extraordinary physical risk, a relationship that Roman society itself appears to have understood and, in its own way, priced accordingly. The prize purses that allowed a Diocles to accumulate a fortune equivalent to a small province's tax revenue, or that allowed a Scorpus to out earn Roman sponsors of considerable independent wealth despite dying before the age of thirty, were not arbitrary figures determined by nothing more than public enthusiasm for the spectacle of racing. They reflected, at least in part, a genuine if never explicitly articulated recognition that an occupation carrying this level of mortal risk required compensation substantial enough to sustain a continuous supply of participants, whether those participants arrived at the profession through the direct compulsion of enslavement or, in the rare cases of free born participants, through a calculated personal decision to accept extraordinary danger in exchange for the possibility of extraordinary reward.

The falx knife, tucked into every charioteer's belt before he ever took the reins, stands as perhaps the single most eloquent piece of physical evidence this book has examined for the true nature of the industry it describes. It was not decorative. It was not symbolic. It was a tool designed for exactly one grim purpose, and its presence on the body of every single charioteer who ever competed at the Circus Maximus or the Hippodrome of Constantinople tells us, more directly than any inscription or literary source could, that the men who built and profited from this financial empire understood precisely what they were asking their charioteers to risk every single time the starting gates opened and the horses surged forward onto the sand.

There is also a broader demographic point worth drawing out explicitly, since it connects the specific evidence this chapter has examined back to the general patterns of Roman mortality discussed earlier in this same chapter. A charioteer who survived his dangerous profession into his thirties or forties, as both Diocles and, in the following chapter's account, Porphyrius eventually did, was beating not only the specific occupational hazards of his profession but the general demographic odds facing any Roman man of his era, odds already substantially shaped, as this chapter noted, by the harsh realities of ancient disease, nutrition, and medicine that shortened lives across every occupation and social class. A successful long career like Diocles' twenty four years therefore represents a double achievement worth appreciating in its full context: survival against both the ordinary mortality risks of life in the Roman world and the specific, dramatically elevated risks of a profession that, as this chapter's opening account of Scorpus illustrates, could and frequently did claim its most talented practitioners well before they reached anything resembling the natural end of an ordinary human lifespan. Viewed against this double burden of risk, the financial rewards this book has documented throughout its preceding chapters look less like simple generous compensation for entertaining the public and more like exactly what this chapter has argued they functioned as: a form of hazard pay, calibrated, however implicitly and however imperfectly, to the genuinely extraordinary mortal stakes the profession demanded of everyone who took up the reins.

The following chapter turns from Rome itself eastward, to Constantinople, tracing how the entire economic and cultural structure this book has described across its preceding chapters transplanted itself into the Byzantine world and reached its final, most spectacularly documented individual expression in the extraordinary career of the sixth century charioteer Porphyrius, a driver whose surviving monuments allow this book to examine, one final time and in unusually rich detail, exactly how the financial machinery of ancient chariot racing rewarded its most exceptional participants.

CHAPTER ELEVEN

PORPHYRIUS AND THE BYZANTINE MACHINE

Seven monuments. That is how many statues the city of Constantinople raised in honor of a single charioteer named Porphyrius, a figure whose active career spanned roughly four decades beginning around the year 500 of the common era, placing him squarely within the same turbulent world of factional politics that would erupt into the catastrophic violence this book examined in its eighth chapter. No other charioteer in the entire surviving record of Roman or Byzantine chariot racing received anything approaching this level of sustained monumental commemoration. Two of these seven monuments survive today, excavated at the site of the old Ottoman court in the nineteenth century and now held in Istanbul's archaeological museums, and their inscriptions, studied most thoroughly by the modern historian Alan Cameron in a landmark scholarly monograph first published in 1973, provide this book with its final and in some ways most revealing case study in the financial and cultural machinery of ancient chariot racing, transplanted by this point in the story from Rome itself to the new imperial capital on the Bosphorus.

By the time Porphyrius began his career, the institutional structure of chariot racing had shifted significantly from the pattern this book traced across its opening chapters, even as its fundamental economic logic remained recognizably intact. The Hippodrome of Constantinople, initially constructed under the emperor Septimius Severus in the early third century and substantially expanded by Constantine when he refounded the city as his new imperial capital in the fourth century, provided the physical stage for this later chapter in the sport's history. Ancient and modern estimates of the Hippodrome's precise seating capacity vary considerably, with figures ranging from thirty thousand at the more conservative end to as high as one hundred thousand at the upper end of scholarly estimation, a genuine range of uncertainty that this book, consistent with its commitment to honest acknowledgment of the limits of available evidence, will not attempt to resolve with false precision. What is not in dispute is the Hippodrome's status as the social and political heart of Constantinople, connected by a private passage directly to the Great Palace itself, through which the emperor could pass directly from his residence into the kathisma, the imperial box overlooking the track, without ever setting foot among the ordinary public thronging the surrounding streets.

This physical connection between palace and racetrack reflects a deeper institutional shift that had occurred in the transition from the Roman system this book examined in its earlier chapters to the Byzantine system Porphyrius competed within. Where the Roman factions of the earlier imperial period, as this book's second chapter detailed, operated as commercial enterprises run by wealthy equestrian entrepreneurs, the Byzantine factions, or demes, had become considerably more formally integrated into the structure of imperial governance itself. Ancient sources describe the demes as effectively linked to specific divisions within Byzantine civic and even senatorial political life, the Blues and Whites generally associated with elements closer to established governmental power, the Greens and Reds carrying a different, often more populist political valence, a formalization of the social and political dimensions of factional identity that this book's earlier chapters observed developing gradually within Roman society but that had, by Porphyrius's era, hardened into something closer to explicit institutional structure.

Porphyrius himself, according to the reconstruction of his career that Cameron's scholarship has established from the surviving inscriptional evidence, achieved something no other charioteer in the surviving record accomplished: formal commemoration from both of the dominant factions of his era, the Blues and the Greens, an achievement that necessarily implies he raced for both factions at different points across his long career, following the same pattern of cross faction movement this book's fifth chapter documented in the career of Diocles nearly four centuries earlier. This detail alone confirms that the competitive market for elite charioteer talent this book identified as a defining feature of the earlier Roman system persisted, in recognizable form, into the very different political and institutional context of sixth century Constantinople, further evidence for the underlying continuity of the sport's essential economic structure even as its surrounding institutional context evolved considerably across the centuries separating Diocles from Porphyrius.

The Hippodrome's central spina, much like its Roman counterpart the Circus Maximus examined in this book's opening chapter, functioned as considerably more than a simple dividing barrier between the two straights of the racing track. Constantine and his successors adorned this central structure with an extraordinary collection of monuments looted or transported from across the empire, most famously the Egyptian obelisk of Theodosius, a genuine pharaonic era monument originally erected at Karnak more than a thousand years before its eventual relocation to Constantinople, mounted on an elaborately carved base depicting the emperor Theodosius presiding over the games from the kathisma. The presence of an authentic ancient Egyptian obelisk, transported across the length of the Mediterranean at what must have been enormous logistical expense and technical difficulty, standing at the center of a racetrack alongside monuments to charioteers like Porphyrius, illustrates something important about how thoroughly the Hippodrome had come to function as a comprehensive stage for the display of accumulated imperial wealth and power, not merely a functional sporting venue. Every monument added to the spina across the centuries, whether an ancient obelisk transported from Egypt, the famous bronze serpent column relocated from the Greek sanctuary at Delphi, or the more modest but still costly statue bases dedicated to celebrated charioteers like Porphyrius, represented a further layer of capital investment justified by the same underlying political logic this book's seventh chapter identified in Roman games funding more broadly: that visible, spectacular expenditure on the shared public space of the racetrack purchased popular goodwill and reinforced imperial legitimacy in a manner that few other categories of state spending could match as efficiently.

The surviving inscriptions commemorating Porphyrius describe a specific and remarkable achievement that appears, based on the current state of scholarly evidence, to have been genuinely unique to his career: victory in what ancient sources call the diversium, a distinctive feature of Byzantine era chariot racing not clearly attested in the same form during the earlier Roman period this book's opening chapters examined. In the diversium, a victorious charioteer would exchange teams with the driver he had just defeated, then compete a second time using his former opponent's own horses, a format explicitly designed to demonstrate that a driver's success reflected genuine individual skill rather than simply the superior quality of the horses fortune had assigned him for a particular race. Winning under these conditions, defeating a rival using that same rival's own team after having already beaten him with one's own, represented a considerably more demanding proof of individual excellence than an ordinary single victory, and the inscriptions commemorating Porphyrius specifically celebrate him as the only charioteer known to have won the diversium twice in a single day, an achievement his contemporary admirers apparently regarded as sufficiently extraordinary to warrant permanent monumental commemoration.

This detail deserves attention beyond its value as an interesting athletic curiosity, because it illuminates something important about how the Byzantine racing establishment approached the challenge of fairly and convincingly evaluating driver talent, a challenge directly relevant to the broader economic argument this book has developed across its preceding chapters. If the factions and their wealthy patrons were investing substantial resources, as this book's earlier chapters demonstrated the Roman factions did, in identifying and developing the most talented available charioteers, they had a direct financial interest in accurately assessing which drivers possessed genuine exceptional skill as opposed to simply having been fortunate enough to drive superior horses in a given race. The diversium format functioned, in effect, as a kind of controlled experiment, isolating driver skill from horse quality by requiring a victorious charioteer to prove his superiority using his opponent's own team, and Porphyrius's specific and unique success in this demanding format provided his patrons and admirers with about as rigorous a demonstration of pure individual talent as the sport's format allowed. This represents a genuine refinement in competitive evaluation methodology compared to the simpler victory statistics this book's fifth chapter documented for Diocles centuries earlier, suggesting an industry that continued to develop and formalize its own internal standards of excellence even as its broader institutional and political context evolved considerably across the intervening centuries.

The relief carvings on Porphyrius's surviving monument bases offer additional, visually striking evidence for exactly how thoroughly Byzantine chariot racing culture had integrated the various threads this book has examined across its preceding chapters, commercial enterprise, imperial political patronage, and passionate popular fandom, into a single coherent public spectacle by the sixth century. The primary relief on one surviving base depicts Porphyrius standing triumphant in his quadriga, a wreath in one hand and either the reins or a palm branch of victory in the other, while surrounding scenes portray his adoring fans, the reigning emperor, likely Anastasius I, observing the spectacle from his position of honor, musicians providing the ceremonial soundtrack to the occasion, and personifications of Victory and of the city of Constantinople itself, depicted holding a cornucopia symbolizing the abundance and prosperity that a successful set of games was understood to represent for the city as a whole. Additional inscribed text on the monument preserves what appear to be genuine crowd chants recorded for posterity, phrases like an exhortation urging on the fortune of the Greens, along with the names of ten specific horses that raced under Porphyrius across his career, a level of specific commemorative detail that echoes, in a Byzantine Greek idiom rather than Roman Latin, the same cultural impulse this book's ninth chapter documented in the graffiti, mosaics, and decorative objects celebrating charioteers and horses across the earlier Roman world.

Porphyrius's monuments did not survive the centuries intact in their original bronze form, a detail that itself carries genuine economic significance worth noting before this chapter turns to the broader decline of chariot racing that its concluding pages will address. The bronze statues that once topped these carefully inscribed stone bases were melted down in the year 1204, during the sack of Constantinople by the forces of the Fourth Crusade, their metal repurposed for the minting of coins amid the general plunder and dismantling of the city's accumulated treasures. Only the stone bases survived this destruction, later removed to the grounds of the Ottoman imperial court following the Turkish conquest of the city in 1453, before eventually entering the collections of Istanbul's archaeological museums where Cameron and subsequent scholars have been able to study them directly. This long and eventful afterlife, from sixth century commission through medieval plunder to eventual modern archaeological preservation, mirrors in its own way the broader arc this book has traced throughout the history of chariot racing as an economic institution: enormous value created, enormous value later destroyed or repurposed by subsequent conquerors and rulers with entirely different priorities, and a final, partial survival owed largely to chance and to the durability of stone where more valuable bronze had long since been melted away.

What Porphyrius's extraordinarily well documented career ultimately demonstrates, considered alongside the broader Byzantine institutional context this chapter has described, is the remarkable persistence of the fundamental economic and cultural logic this book identified in its opening chapters examining the Roman Circus Maximus, even as that logic adapted itself to a new capital, a new and more formalized relationship between the factions and imperial governance, and refined competitive formats like the diversium that pushed the evaluation of driver talent to new levels of rigor. The financial empire this book has traced from the muddy floodplain between Rome's Aventine and Palatine hills had, by the sixth century, transplanted itself successfully to the shores of the Bosphorus, sustaining substantially the same essential structure of faction competition, driver celebrity, public subsidy, and passionate popular identification across a gap of many centuries and a considerable shift in the empire's political center of gravity from west to east.

It is worth pausing, finally, on the practical mechanics of how a career like Porphyrius's four decade span in active competition would have functioned within the Byzantine faction system this chapter has described. A driver active across roughly forty years, an unusually long career even by the standards of Diocles' already exceptional twenty four years examined in this book's fifth chapter, would have required his patron faction or factions to maintain an extraordinary and sustained commitment of resources across an equally extraordinary span of time: successive generations of horses bred, trained, and eventually retired around him, successive faction managers and owners who inherited responsibility for his continued support, and a continuous public appetite for his particular driving style and tactical reputation that somehow renewed itself across four decades of Constantinople's notoriously fickle and passionate sporting public. That Porphyrius achieved this, and that his patrons across both the Blue and Green factions evidently judged the continued investment worthwhile across such an unusually long span, offers this book's final and perhaps most striking piece of evidence for just how deeply embedded the economic logic of sustained investment in proven charioteer talent, first documented in this book's earlier chapters examining the Roman system, remained within the very different institutional context of sixth century Byzantium.

Yet even as Porphyrius's monuments testify to the continued vitality of this system in the sixth century, the seeds of its eventual decline were already present in the very events this book's eighth chapter examined in detail, the catastrophic Nika riots that nearly toppled Justinian's reign and that prompted subsequent emperors to view the accumulated political power of the racing demes with far greater wariness than their predecessors had generally displayed. The following chapter, the final chapter of this book's main narrative, turns to that eventual decline, tracing the gradual economic and cultural forces that brought many centuries of sustained investment in chariot racing to its eventual close, and considering what the entire arc of this history, from muddy Roman floodplain to abandoned Byzantine hippodrome, ultimately teaches us about the relationship between spectacle, money, and power that has proven so durable across the whole of human history since.

CHAPTER TWELVE

THE LEDGER CLOSES

Empires do not usually end with a bang. Roman chariot racing, an industry that had sustained itself across nearly a thousand years of recorded history, generating fortunes for faction owners, breeders, and charioteers alike while consuming a share of public and private wealth that this book has argued rivaled almost any other category of ancient economic activity, did not end in any single dramatic moment either. It faded, region by region and century by century, as the underlying economic and political conditions that had sustained it for so long gradually eroded, until an industry that had once commanded the devoted attention of a quarter of a million spectators in a single Roman afternoon dwindled into occasional, increasingly ceremonial events staged in a single surviving hippodrome, and then, eventually, into nothing at all.

The decline began, as this book's earlier chapters have already suggested, in the western half of the Roman Empire considerably earlier than in the east. As the political and economic structures of the western Empire fractured across the fifth century, the elaborate network of public funding this book's seventh chapter described in such detail, the aediles and their successors, the imperial subsidies, the summa honoraria payments extracted from provincial civic magistrates, could no longer be sustained at anything resembling its former scale. Individual circuses across the western provinces, many of them substantial structures in their own right even if none approached the scale of the Circus Maximus itself, gradually ceased operating as the cities that had once funded them lost population, wealth, and, in many cases, effective governmental continuity amid the broader political fragmentation of the fifth century west. Rome itself continued to host chariot races for a time even after the formal end of the western imperial line in 476, sustained first under Ostrogothic rule and later by other authorities including, eventually, the papacy, which found in the continued funding of public spectacle the same basic political logic that Roman emperors had exploited for centuries: an investment in popular entertainment purchased popular goodwill considerably more reliably than most alternative uses of the same resources. But the scale of these later western races never approached the heights the sport had achieved during the height of Roman imperial power, and the Circus Maximus itself gradually fell out of active use as a competitive venue across the sixth century, a casualty of the broader economic and political collapse that accompanied the prolonged and devastating conflict historians call the Gothic Wars.

The eastern half of the empire, centered on Constantinople and possessing considerably greater sustained economic and political stability than the fragmenting west, preserved chariot racing in something closer to its full historical vigor for a longer period, a continuity this book's eleventh chapter traced through the extraordinary career of Porphyrius in the early sixth century. Yet even in the east, the seeds of eventual decline were already visible in the very events this book's eighth chapter examined in detail. The Nika riots of 532, whatever their immediate political resolution in Justinian's favor, demonstrated with unmistakable clarity the genuine danger that the accumulated political power of the racing factions posed to imperial stability, and subsequent Byzantine emperors, while continuing to fund and attend chariot racing as an important instrument of public governance in the tradition this book's seventh chapter described, generally approached the factions with somewhat greater institutional wariness than their predecessors had displayed before 532 forced the danger into unmistakable view.

The seventh century brought challenges to the Byzantine Empire that went well beyond concerns about factional political power, and these broader challenges proved decisive in bringing the long history of large scale chariot racing to its eventual close. A prolonged and costly war against Sassanid Persia strained imperial finances considerably, and this strain was compounded, catastrophically, by the rapid Arab conquests that began in the 630s, which stripped the Byzantine Empire of Egypt, Syria, and eventually most of North Africa in a remarkably short span of years. These territories had represented enormous sources of imperial revenue, and their loss struck directly at the financial foundation that had sustained lavish public spectacle across the eastern Mediterranean for centuries. Cities beyond Constantinople itself, many of which had maintained their own local circuses and racing traditions in the pattern this book's earlier chapters described, increasingly could not sustain the expense, and provincial chariot racing outside the imperial capital contracted sharply across the middle decades of the seventh century, in many places disappearing entirely as the broader urban economic base that had once supported it shrank or vanished altogether amid the empire's mounting territorial and financial crises.

Religious change compounded these economic and military pressures, though the relationship between Christian institutional authority and the survival of chariot racing proves, on closer examination, considerably more complicated than a simple narrative of religious suppression would suggest. Christian writers and church leaders had criticized public spectacle, chariot racing very much included, since at least the height of the Roman imperial period, objecting to what they regarded as the sport's pagan religious origins, examined in this book's opening chapter, and to the excessive passions, financial and emotional alike, that the races provoked among the Christian faithful. The fourth century bishop John Chrysostom delivered a specific homily in the year 399 directly criticizing the games and their effect on public Christian morality, yet contemporary evidence indicates his criticism achieved little practical effect on actual public attendance or behavior, with the races continuing to draw enormous crowds despite consistent ecclesiastical disapproval stretching across several centuries. This suggests that religious opposition alone, however consistently expressed by Christian authorities over a very long period, was not in itself sufficient to end the sport's popularity. It required the additional, and ultimately decisive, pressure of the genuine economic and military crises of the seventh century to finally undermine an institution that had proven remarkably resilient against purely moral or religious criticism across many previous centuries of recorded Christian objection.

Constantinople itself, benefiting from its unusually defensible location and its continued status as the seat of whatever remained of Byzantine imperial authority, preserved chariot racing longer than any other city in the former Roman world, though increasingly the financial burden of sustaining even this reduced scale of racing fell more heavily on direct imperial funding rather than the broader network of private and civic patronage that had once distributed the cost of public spectacle across a far wider base of wealthy participants throughout the empire. The races that continued in Constantinople across the seventh, eighth, and ninth centuries increasingly took on a more explicitly ceremonial character, this book's eleventh chapter having already noted the gradual shift toward the sport's diminished cultural relevance beginning around the seventh century, with racing increasingly subordinated to broader imperial ritual and processional display rather than functioning as the primary, independently significant public entertainment institution it had represented during the height of Roman and early Byzantine power.

The final chapter of this long decline came with the sack of Constantinople by the forces of the Fourth Crusade in the year 1204, an event this book's eleventh chapter already noted in connection with the melting down of Porphyrius's bronze statues for coinage. The Hippodrome itself suffered extensive damage and looting during this catastrophic episode, and while a diminished

Byzantine state eventually recovered control of Constantinople and continued to exist for several more centuries, chariot racing on anything resembling its former imperial scale never resumed. The institution that had once organized an enormous share of the ancient Mediterranean economy, sustained fortunes for faction owners and successful charioteers alike, and shaped the political and social life of two successive imperial capitals across nearly a thousand years, simply ceased to exist as an ongoing, economically significant enterprise, its physical remains gradually buried, built over, or, in the case of the Circus Maximus itself, reduced to the grassy public park that occupies the site in modern Rome today.

The physical site of the Circus Maximus itself experienced its own long afterlife following the end of active racing, one that mirrors in microcosm the broader arc of decline and transformation this chapter has traced across the wider institution. Freed from its original function, the valley between the Aventine and Palatine hills gradually reverted, across the medieval centuries, to a far more modest existence, its once monumental stone tiers quarried away over time by later builders seeking ready cut material for other construction projects across the city, a common fate for major Roman structures once their original purpose had lapsed and their accumulated stone became, in the eyes of a shrinking medieval population with far more modest building ambitions than the emperors who had first raised the Circus, simply a convenient and cost free source of building material. Vegetable gardens, small scale agriculture, and eventually industrial uses occupied the site across various points in its long medieval and early modern history, the space's original function as the largest entertainment venue the ancient world had ever constructed passing gradually out of active local memory even as classical scholars and antiquarians continued to study its history from surviving literary sources. Modern archaeological investigation across the nineteenth and twentieth centuries gradually recovered and confirmed much of what ancient authors had described, and the site today functions as public parkland, its long grassy oval still clearly tracing the outline of the ancient track for any visitor who takes the time to look, a quiet and largely unmarked survival of an institution that once commanded the sustained attention and financial investment of an entire empire.

What should we make, in the end, of this long and genuinely remarkable history? This book opened with a promise to restore the hidden financial machinery of Roman chariot racing to view, and across its preceding eleven chapters it has attempted to do exactly that: tracing the physical scale of the Circus Maximus itself, the corporate structure of the four racing factions and their equestrian owners, the international breeding networks that supplied circus quality horses from Hispania to Cappadocia, the brutal but genuinely lucrative labor market for enslaved and eventually freed charioteers, the almost unbelievable individual fortune documented in Diocles' carefully inscribed career earnings, the informal but economically significant betting economy revealed most vividly through buried curse tablets, the enormous public and private expenditure that emperors and civic magistrates alike poured into funding games as a deliberate instrument of political governance, the catastrophic destructive potential of factional loyalty demonstrated by the Nika riots, the vast informal economy of popular fan culture and material commemoration, the constant mortal risk that shadowed even the most celebrated careers, and finally the sport's remarkable transplantation to Constantinople and its long, gradual decline across the seventh through thirteenth centuries.

The picture that emerges from this full arc of history is not simply a curious footnote to more conventional accounts of Roman political and military history, gladiators and emperors and legions marching across provincial frontiers. It is evidence of something this book has argued deserves genuine reconsideration: that ancient societies, for all the vast technological and institutional differences separating them from the modern world, developed commercial, financial, and celebrity driven entertainment industries considerably more sophisticated and economically consequential than popular modern imagination typically credits them with achieving. The domini factionum who ran the Roman racing stables were businessmen operating complex, capital intensive, multinational commercial enterprises. The breeding networks that supplied their horses functioned as genuine international supply chains, coordinated across thousands of miles of Mediterranean trade routes. The charioteers themselves, most beginning their careers enslaved, participated in a labor market whose extreme risks and extraordinary potential rewards bear a genuinely uncomfortable resemblance to modern debates about athlete compensation, occupational hazard, and the ethics of extracting extraordinary value from individuals whose initial entry into a dangerous profession was never fully voluntary. And the public funding structures that sustained the entire apparatus, from individual aediles competing for popular favor in the late Republic through emperors calculating the political returns on lavish imperial games, represent a genuinely sophisticated understanding, however different in its specific mechanisms from modern public finance, of the relationship between public entertainment spending and political legitimacy.

Diocles' inscription, carved in stone nearly nineteen centuries ago, still stands as perhaps the single most eloquent piece of evidence this book has examined for just how seriously, and how precisely, the Romans themselves understood and valued the financial dimensions of their chariot racing industry. A man born into slavery in a Roman province, who spent twenty four years risking his life in an occupation that killed a great many of his contemporaries before they reached middle age, left behind a monument that reads, in its granular precision and evident pride, remarkably like a modern professional athlete's carefully compiled career statistics, complete with prize money broken down by category and tactical victories itemized by type. That such a document survives at all, carved by a man whose origins placed him at the very bottom of Roman society's formal hierarchy of status, and that it survives specifically because Diocles himself understood his own financial and athletic achievement as worthy of permanent commemoration, tells us something genuinely important about how Roman society, for all its formal prejudices against commerce and against the enslaved and formerly enslaved individuals who so often conducted it, nonetheless recognized and rewarded exceptional individual achievement within this particular, extraordinarily lucrative corner of its economy.

The valley between the Aventine and Palatine hills is a public park today, walked by tourists who may notice the long, low outline of the ancient track beneath the grass without necessarily appreciating the full scale of the financial empire that once operated there. This book has tried to restore some measure of that appreciation, not merely as an antiquarian curiosity but as a genuine contribution to how we understand the economic sophistication of the ancient world more broadly. The dust of the Circus Maximus settled many centuries ago. The ledgers, where they survive at all, are scattered across scholarly monographs, museum collections, and the patient work of archaeologists and epigraphers piecing together fragments of stone and lead. But the story they tell, of horses bred for fortunes, of enslaved boys who became millionaires, of curses buried in desperate hope of altering a race's outcome, and of an entire imperial economy organized in significant part around the simple, thundering spectacle of four horse teams racing around a track, deserves to be told with the same seriousness modern readers extend to any other major chapter of ancient economic history. Rome ran on more than legions and grain. For nearly a thousand years, it ran on speed, and on the money that speed, brilliantly and ruthlessly organized, never stopped generating.

EPILOGUE: WHAT THE CIRCUS STILL TEACHES

A modern reader closing this book might reasonably ask what practical relevance any of it holds beyond the genuine pleasure of a good historical story well told. The Circus Maximus is gone. The four factions have not fielded a chariot in well over a thousand years. Diocles, Scorpus, and Porphyrius are names known today only to specialists and to readers who have just spent several hundred pages in their company. Why should any of this matter to someone living in a world of televised football leagues, franchise valuations, and athlete endorsement deals that would have been unimaginable to a Roman faction owner however shrewd his own commercial instincts?

The answer, this epilogue argues, lies less in any specific parallel between ancient and modern sport, though this book has drawn several such parallels along the way, and more in a broader lesson about the durability of certain basic economic and social patterns whenever a society organizes large scale public entertainment around competitive spectacle, individual celebrity, and passionate collective identification. Modern professional sports leagues, for all their vastly greater technological sophistication and global reach, rest on a remarkably similar foundation to the one this book has spent its preceding chapters excavating from beneath the Circus Maximus: a labor market in which a small number of extraordinarily talented individuals command extraordinary compensation while facing genuine physical risk, a commercial apparatus of team ownership and management that captures and redistributes the majority of the wealth this labor generates, an intense and often irrational public loyalty cultivated deliberately through decades of consistent brand identity, a betting economy that exists in constantly shifting relationship to the sport's formal governing structures, and a persistent, mutually beneficial relationship between the sport's organizers and the political authorities who find in public spectacle a genuinely useful instrument of governance and popular goodwill.

None of this should be taken to suggest that history simply repeats itself in some deterministic fashion, or that a modern sports executive has anything specific to learn from the operational playbook of a second century Roman faction owner. The differences between ancient and modern sporting economies are, in most particulars, at least as significant as the similarities, and this book has tried throughout to resist the temptation of forcing ancient evidence into an artificially tidy modern framework where the historical record itself supports a more complicated and less convenient picture. What this book does suggest, and what this epilogue wants to leave as its final and most durable point, is that the underlying human appetites, for competitive spectacle, for individual celebrity, for collective identity built around shared loyalty to a color or a symbol, and for the particular thrill of risking something valuable on an uncertain outcome, are considerably older and more stable across historical time than the specific technological and institutional forms through which any given society happens to satisfy them.

Rome built the largest entertainment venue the ancient world would ever see because its people wanted exactly what people continue wanting today: the chance to watch extraordinary individuals compete at the absolute limit of human and animal capability, to feel the collective surge of a shared identity cheering a beloved color or team toward victory, and to have something, however small, riding personally on how that competition turned out. The Romans organized the satisfaction of that appetite into an industry of genuine financial sophistication, sustained across nearly a thousand years and two successive imperial capitals, and this book has tried to give that industry, and the largely forgotten individuals, breeders, faction owners, curse tablet writers, and above all the charioteers themselves, who built and populated it, the serious economic history it has long deserved and too rarely received.

The next time a modern reader watches any contest of speed and skill played out before a roaring crowd, with fortunes and reputations riding on the outcome, they might spare a thought for the valley between two Roman hills where an industry built on exactly these same human appetites once reached a scale and sophistication that would not be matched again for the better part of two thousand years. The dust has long since settled over the Circus Maximus, but the ledger it kept, however scattered and fragmentary its surviving pages, still has a great deal to teach us about who we are, and about what we have always, it seems, been willing to pay to watch.

A NOTE ON SOURCES

This book rests on a combination of ancient primary evidence and modern scholarship, and readers interested in exploring the subject further may find the following starting points useful.

The single most important primary source for the material in this book is the inscription commemorating the charioteer Gaius Appuleius Diocles, cataloged as Corpus Inscriptionum Latinarum, volume six, number 10048, erected in the year 146 of the common era and examined in detail in this book's fifth chapter. The Roman agricultural writer Columella, particularly the sixth book of his De Re Rustica, provides essential evidence for the classification and breeding of circus horses discussed in this book's third chapter. The satirist Juvenal, especially his tenth Satire, remains the source of the phrase panem et circenses examined in this book's seventh chapter, while the epigrammatist Martial offers scattered but valuable references to famous charioteers and horses throughout his surviving work. For the Byzantine period covered in this book's eleventh and twelfth chapters, the contemporary historian Procopius, particularly his account of the Nika riots, and the chronicler John Malalas provide the essential ancient narrative sources, supplemented by the epigraphic evidence from Porphyrius's surviving monument bases.

Among modern scholarly works, Alan Cameron's Porphyrius the Charioteer, first published in 1973, remains the foundational study of its subject and the essential starting point for any reader wishing to explore the Byzantine charioteer's career in greater depth than this book's eleventh chapter allows. The extensive corpus of circus curse tablets recovered from Hadrumetum and Carthage, discussed in this book's sixth chapter, was first systematically published by Auguste Audollent in his Defixionum Tabellae, and subsequent scholarship on this material continues to refine our understanding of the practice. Readers interested in the broader institution of Roman public games and their funding, the subject of this book's seventh chapter, will find useful material in the substantial modern literature on Roman ludi and the office of the aedileship. The demographic evidence underlying this book's tenth chapter draws on the long tradition of scholarly analysis of Roman epitaph inscriptions, a field shaped significantly by the foundational work of scholars including John Durand and Keith Hopkins, whose methodological cautions about the limitations of tombstone evidence this book has tried to observe carefully throughout.

Archaeological and epigraphic evidence for the Circus Maximus itself, discussed in this book's opening chapter, has been synthesized across numerous excavation reports and topographical studies of ancient Rome, while the material culture of fan identification examined in this book's ninth chapter, mosaics, graffiti, and everyday decorative objects, has been documented extensively in regional archaeological surveys, particularly of Roman North Africa, where this evidence survives in unusually rich concentration.

Where this book has offered a specific numerical figure, a date, a career statistic, or a direct quotation from an ancient source, it has done so on the basis of evidence attested in the sources described above. Where the evidence is genuinely ambiguous or contested among modern scholars, this book has tried to say so directly rather than presenting a false certainty the historical record does not support. Any errors of interpretation that remain are the author's own.

ABOUT THE AUTHOR

Marcus Verdineau writes narrative history focused on the hidden economic machinery behind moments the popular imagination remembers mainly for their spectacle. Trained in classical history before moving into long form nonfiction writing, Verdineau specializes in the kind of archival and epigraphic research that rarely makes it past academic journals into books written for a general audience, translating inscriptions, legal texts, and archaeological reports into narrative history that keeps the underlying evidence honest while remaining genuinely readable. Circus Economics reflects an abiding interest in the ancient world's commercial life, the merchants, breeders, laborers, and financiers whose work rarely survives in the historical record with the same clarity as the emperors and generals who have traditionally dominated popular accounts of antiquity. Verdineau continues to research and write about the economic undercurrents of the ancient Mediterranean world.

www.ingramcontent.com/pod-product-compliance
Lightning Source LLC
LaVergne TN
LVHW100145061126
851857LV00010B/248
* 9 7 9 8 2 3 5 0 3 7 4 2 7 *